Programmed to HATE

Homosexuality & Me.

My true story of
Conversion Therapy

Matthew Gordon

2022

Introduction

I want to begin by expressing that this is a true story. This is
my own and deeply personal story. The story of my life,
experiences, and my pursuit of happiness. I am choosing to
write about this as a form of self-guided therapy as I attempt
to free myself from the pain of my past. I've never been able
to tell this story to anyone. I've never had anyone who would
listen or anyone who would care to hear these words. Beyond
never having anyone to tell, my story had too much power
over me, my actions, and my thoughts. I have always wanted
to get past this trauma but I have never had a path forward
or a workable solution. With any luck, this is going to help
me to improve my own quality of life and improve my mental
health. Although I am writing my story and sharing it here as
a form of healing, I also hope that my story can help others.
Perhaps my story may even help to avoid painful paths.

The world today is filled with discussion and debate which
fundamentally focus on childhood development, sexual
orientation and gender identity, and a host of related topics

which are similar to my own lived experiences. I believe that by sharing my story here I can help shed some light onto these important matters and perhaps help to protect children through enlightening others. My only ambitions or desires here are to heal, to help, and to hopefully prevent the proliferation of abuse.

I've chosen to write this story under a pseudonym. Where particular details may have revealed my true name or identity, or the identities of others who are crucial figures in my story, I have deliberately omitted such specifics or included creative alterations to maintain anonymity. Telling this story is about healing, not exacerbating any hurt feelings or bringing ridicule or shame onto others. I hope that I am able to provide something meaningful to readers who may be suffering from the same or similar types of trauma to heal as well. That is my goal – healing.

I would ask that all readers respect my need for anonymity, as well as the anonymity of those included in my life story. Some day in the future I may be strong enough to sign my real name to this story. I'm simply not strong enough, yet. In time, I will be healed enough to be out in the open. Please respect that I'm not yet ready to out myself.

This story contains depictions of child sexual activity, homophobia, suicidal ideation, abuse, addiction and self-harm.

Now, allow me to begin telling my life story, unfiltered, unedited and singularly told on my own. It's just me and the laptop keyboard now…

Chapter 1
Genesis of Trauma

God hates fags. Let those words run through your mind, your heart, and soul. Ask yourself if you had a physiological response to reading those three short words. I did. I felt it in my stomach, gut, and my jaw. Those three little words have so much power in them.

God: an omnipotent all-powerful being of unlimited authority and capacity for any, all, and everything.
Hate(s): an uncontrollable loathing for something abhorrent.
Fags: a slur. An insult. A discriminatory derogation against persons for their sexual orientation.

Three little words. Yet, for me, such an overwhelming source of stress, hurt, and despair. For me, the horrendous slogan "God hates fags" is a programming that was forced upon me as a child. I didn't choose it, though, I am deeply ashamed to admit that out of fear I allowed that programming to take root. I allowed it to infect my inner thoughts. It was not simply a form of programming but it was a virus of thought. It entered my system and derailed my mind from normal operating procedure. The person who I was meant to become was forever and irretrievably lost to that deliberate programming of how my mind would work. It is programming which has caused me immeasurable pain, sorrow, and misery. The pain is so great that I've spent my entire life using proverbial Band-Aids to keep it all together.

I want to be perfectly clear that this is my true story. It isn't something I wrote to amuse or entertain strangers online. Far from it. I'm not a professional writer and actually, I find communicating to be rather difficult. I simply have to write my story and share it. My story is so painful that it borders upon debilitating. Hopefully that will soon change. Hopefully I'm on a journey toward healing.

I'm stalling. Can you feel it? My own story holds so much power over me that I'm afraid to even type it out.

I believe in God. I believe there is a spiritual force which neither I, nor anyone else, can explain. I believe this holy spirit is capable of great things. I believe the holy spirit brings comfort to those in times of desperation. I believe the holy spirit will bring wisdom, clarity, or strength in dark times to those who need it. I believe in these things because in several instances in my life I have felt that godly presence. I'll get to some of those experiences in due course. First I need to clarify that the God that I believe in is not the Sky Santa depicted by major religious groups. I do not believe that a being so powerful that it created Earth, the solar system, the galaxy, a billion other galaxies, a universe of inconceivable vastness and complexity could ever be so weak as to have time and energy for hatred.

God does not have time nor the inclination to *hate* anyone.

I have spent a lifetime pondering God. As you will see, I spent a great deal of time dwelling upon my need for understanding of God. Finally, I am arriving at the point at which I can comfortably conclude that God doesn't hate. Weak-minded people have hatred. Ascribing their own hatred to God is simply a marketing ploy. The ultimate appeal to authority.

I grew up in a small little place that's out of the way and out of the minds of most people in the modern world. It's the ultimate small town. If you aren't from nearby, you've never heard of the place I call home. Growing up there were only a few kids my age in that small community. I was friends with two slightly older boys. Actually, they were my only friends. Although it was an ultra conservative, old fashioned conservative town, my family managed to stand out as outlier zealots.

My family was ultra religious. We went to church every Sunday. We dressed in clothing which was easily more than a decade behind the fashion of everyone else in our town. The teachings of the Bible were an important element of daily life. As far as my family was concerned, my only two friends in the world weren't good enough. They were too lowly and sinful. Their families didn't go to church. They watched television shows on the Sabbath – a crime if ever there was one. Those families may even have allowed their kids to use unacceptable language like the word "poop."

I was discouraged from having real friends and was instead pushed toward religious activities. Not only was I discouraged from having friends or playing games with other kids but my parents went to great lengths to ensure I was socially isolated from my peers. I wasn't allowed to dress myself or to choose my own clothing. If I had been allowed, I'd have dressed the way the other kids my age dressed. Instead I was forced to wear those outdated dress clothes to any and every event. Even as a five year old I completely despised being forcibly 'othered' all of the time. One of my earliest memories is of smuggling t-shirts to school in my backpack. It was first grade and I was already struggling to have my own identity, my own sense of self.

On the school bus I changed from a bulky collared shirt into a t-shirt. I remember feeling liberated and free. I was then at least partially dressed the same as the other kids. Dressed somewhat like the other kids, I was happy and excited to get to school. I just wanted to fit in. I just wanted to be normal. It's what everyone wants in their school years, yet, for me it was a battle right out of the gate. Right from the early days of first grade I was being isolated, othered, and set categorically apart from my peers. It bothered me so much that as an otherwise obedient child, I was smuggling contraband t-shirts to school.

I don't remember how my parents found out that I'd changed shirts at school but I do remember that they were furious. Furious with a first-grader for wearing a t-shirt at school. A t-shirt that, knowing my family, probably had a picture of the Bible on it for all I know. None of that mattered, though. My parents found out and they took the t-shirt away from me. They began inspecting my backpack to ensure I couldn't have that small opportunity for individualism ever again.

Being able to choose your own clothing, your own style of clothes, and determine your own comfort needs are very, very basic human dignities. I didn't have that. It seemed that everyone else around me, aside from my siblings, did have that dignity. Not being able to wear what you want to wear because of religion or tyrannical authority figures who just want to undermine your sense of self damages a child's development. At least in my experience it did. It's not like I wanted to wear a bathing suit to church or a clown shirt to a funeral. I wanted to wear reasonably comparable types of clothing to my peers and not be ostracized by other children for being so visibly different. For my parents, that was not only too much to ask, it was an affront to their religion.

My parents knew that I just wanted to fit in. They knew that not wearing the same clothing as my peers was a sticking point for me. I had been something of a happy-go-lucky kid who only wanted to run around and play games and have fun with the other kids my age. I will never understand why being a happy five or six or seven year old is such an offense, or why I'd ever be punished for having energy and enthusiasm for life.

My happy, energetic, freedom-loving spirit had certainly drawn the ire of my parents. I wanted to wear t-shirts and flexible pants. They wanted me dressed in buttoned-up collared shirts and ill-fitted wool trousers at all times. The more I protested, the more ill-fitted those wool trousers seemed to become. But even that wasn't enough. One weekend we were headed off to a family reunion event. I wanted to bring sneakers to run and play around. Rather than acquiesce to that request, my parents went in the opposite direction.

They dressed me in a pair of my sister's panties. I wish I were kidding but I'm not. They dressed me in pink and white frilly panties to go to a family reunion. Forgive me for not clearly remembering the shirt or the pants but I'm quite confident those were outdated, ill-fitted, and smelled like an old attic. Because that's how I was forced to appear to the world at all times. That day as a child, I remember feeling disgraced and humiliated. Not that my feelings meant anything to anyone. That was an unfortunate recurring theme for me.

In the summer months my parents would let us do one 'fun' thing each summer. In those early years it was usually an afternoon at an amusement park in a town about an hour away. There was one such summer 'fun day' that I'll never forget. I was about 7 years old. Finally, they were going to take us to the amusement park. Not surprisingly for me at that age, I wanted to wear comfortable shorts and a t-shirt so that I could be free and able to run around like a normal kid. Yet, once again, that wasn't what my parents wanted for me. Even on the so-called summer 'fun day.' The one day of the year when I'm supposedly allowed to have fun. Even on that special day they dressed me as though I was going to church to read a sacred script before an adoring audience.

Even on 'fun day' I wasn't allowed to be myself or even to feel comfortable. I'll remember this discomfort for the rest of my life. That day my parents forced me to wear shorts that were not only too small but they rode up between my testicles, tightly cutting up into me like barbed wire. I yet again protested being forced to wear such uncomfortable and ill-suited clothing. It isn't like my family didn't have t-shirts or gym shorts. Those garments were absolutely accessible and within our home. I simply wasn't allowed to wear them.

My balls were being squeezed. I was in a state beyond discomfort. I was in pain. I didn't know the correct anatomical phrases to use but I made it clear that I was totally uncomfortable. These are parents who once forced me to wear panties simply to teach me not to complain about how I've been dressed. Perhaps unsurprisingly then, my parents said that either I would go to the amusement park in the ball-crushing tight shorts or that I would not get to participate in the 'fun day' that summer. That is some decidedly Old Testament parenting on display, where one must have their testicles squeezed and bruised before any fun may be permitted.

When I say that this was the only 'fun day' in the summer, I truly mean that. My parents had me working harder than a fully grown carpenter or tradesperson my entire life. At that age, even around 7 years old, I had callouses on the palms of my hands. Think to yourself when is the last time you shook hands with a person whose palm was dry and breaking with calloused skin. That was me at age 7. So, for whatever reason, I chose to still attend the 'fun day' despite the horrendous squeezing of my balls in those ridiculous shorts. Admittedly, I regretted that decision the whole day. No bumper-cart that moves at half the speed of a ride-on lawnmower can compensate for the testicular pain inflicted upon me that day.

That actually sums up my childhood fairly succinctly. Neither the event nor activity mattered. My spirit was being crushed at every opportunity. Believe me when I say that I was never allowed to be an individual with my own sense of identity. Laughter was frowned upon at best, and could sometimes bring a hard smack. Playfulness was equated with badness. Self-expression was a sin. Daring to dream, to aspire, to fantasize about becoming successful in life, was all an insult to those around me. Expressing the slightest hope would bring about a hurricane of negativity. No you can't do that. No you can't be that. No you can't accomplish that. No you can't succeed at that. No you won't be anyone important, respectable, or happy. No, you won't ever matter.

I can hear them now. Even in my thirties, I can hear them now as clear as day. They've said it to me so many times, in so many situations, so monotonously. I can hear them cutting me down from any aspiration, anywhere, always.

Being so restricted and pushed down by all of their negativity made me wildly unhappy. I felt awkward, lonely and oppressed. Even if I didn't have the terminology for it until later in life, I know how I felt, and I know what those feelings were. I felt like I was being cut off at the knees by my own family in the great walk of life. Each of us has a journey to walk. Some are privileged from the beginning. Others are not. Yet some others, like me, are figuratively cut off at the knees by their own family. That's how my life began. That was my beginning on the great journey of my life.

Now comes the hard part of my story. This is the part where I break down in uncontrollable tears and devolve into a panic attack. This is the part that I can't say out loud without choking on my words. My memory here is fragmented. I've spent a lifetime trying to forget and to erase these memories from existence. So forgive me when I say that I believe that I was still 7 years old. It's possible, given the other events going on around the time of these memories, that I was perhaps as old as 9. All that I can do is narrow it down to that window. I obviously did not take contemporaneous notes. All that I have is my own memory. But I'll tell you everything that I can remember.

I was with the two older boys in my community. The two boys who were my only real friends. We were running around playing games. We often ran off into the woods to get away from adult supervision. We played games like 'cops and robbers' or 'tag' or we pretended there were mystical wild animals chasing us. It was all pretty harmless. Nothing but innocent childish games. Until it wasn't. As I slowly allow this memory to come back to the surface I feel a tightness in my chest. My stomach has clenched and churned. My heart is beating faster, simply from this memory beginning to rise to the surface.

This memory haunts me in a way that I believe this is how people who have run over innocent children with their cars must feel.

We were just innocent kids in the woods. I think we were pretending a wolf was on the loose and chasing us. Whatever it was, we were only playing as we brought ourselves further into the bushes and trees. We weren't all that far from where we could be easily found but we were out of direct sight. I don't know how we went from pretending we were being chased by a wolf to 'a different game.' I can't recall the transitional events. It simply went from one activity to the other. We weren't running around anymore. We were standing still as a group. The other boys pulled their shorts down and began fondling their genitals.

My memory is blank on how it all started but soon the three of us were engaged in – and the tears are flowing now – sex. We were all lined up. I was at the front of the line. One of the other boys had anally penetrated me with his penis. Behind him, he also was being anally penetrated. The three of us were having gay sex. Male-to-male-to-male sex.

At that time in my life my vocabulary did not include words such as "penis," "sex," "gay", nor anything approximating such terms. I did not know what sex even was. I didn't know what we were doing or the significance of any of it. I was simply too young and sheltered to have any inkling of what this 'game' truly was.

The other boys were laughing. Not in a sinister way; I'm not calling them rapists. I have no idea what their level of understanding of these acts may have been. I just know that for them there was nothing to be feared from this activity. They were freely having fun and laughing. I remember them laughing. I wasn't. I didn't laugh. I didn't know what this was. This activity may have gone on for several minutes or perhaps it was mere seconds. I don't know. I can't completely remember it. Though, I do remember what happened next.

We were in the bushes and nobody could see us. Yet we were only fifty feet or so from the road. Suddenly I became aware that my parents were walking down the road. *My parents.* Those old-timey Christian zealots who would rather bruise you than allow you to wear a t-shirt and gender-appropriate underwear. Whether they were specifically coming to find me in that instant or merely trying to approximately note our location in the woods I suppose I'll never know. I panicked. I didn't know what we were doing but I knew that my parents could never find out about it. Everything about it felt like something that needed to be hidden, concealed, and certainly kept from my family. Whatever this was it surely would draw an angry tirade from my tyrannical, overbearing ultra-religious parents. That thought was imprinted into my brain as a sense of fear set in.

I pulled my clothes back on and started to run. I needed to get away from whatever had just happened. I needed to escape that moment and never look back. I immediately felt a sense of deep shame, humiliation, embarrassment, and *terror*. I was absolutely terrified. It was a genuine, palpable, punishing form of terror. The one thing that I did know was that I needed to keep this secret for the rest of my life. I could never tell anyone what had happened. Neither my parents nor anyone else in my family could ever know. Which thereupon began my own internal psychological fortifications and compartmentalizations. I built barriers around that event in my memory. I isolated parts of my mind and kept that part of me hidden, separated, and secret. Should any of those thoughts or memories ever rise to the surface I'd beat those thoughts and feelings away. I pushed them down hard, far, into the depths of my soul.

This event was something I never wanted anyone to know about. I didn't want it to ever be revealed to anyone. I buried the memory. I buried it so deep that not even I could find it. My own childhood memories remained a secret from my conscious mind for over two decades.

Chapter 2
Preaching Hate

My parents befriended members of an extreme religious cult. No, I'm not just being dramatic. I truly believe they meet at least the colloquial definition of a cult. Allow me to expand on that comment. My parents befriended an exceptionally large family of religious extremists whose dogma and isolationist views, to me, were cult-like. This cultish family came into our lives while I was still around the age of 7-9 years in my childhood. No doubt, you're noticing a theme for me. The years around 7-9 years old. Indeed, that's where it happened. That's where my real story of trauma begins. My frame of reference to accurately calibrate my age at the time of these events is broad. So to ensure I'm telling my story as truthfully as I can, I'm not going to get specific on 7, 8, or 9 years of age. I don't know how much that would change, anyway. Reasonable people will understand, though, that giving the range of 7-9 years ought to be a close enough approximation for what I am about to describe.

I remember that I never liked this ultra religious cult family. I was a kid and I just wanted to have fun. These people weren't any fun. They were the antithesis of fun. They had peculiar rules governing their attire and appearance. They wore suspenders, not belts. Women in their little cult wore dresses down to the ankle, never pants. Their hair was long enough to practically touch the floor. They didn't own televisions or radios and while your grandmother might think Lady Gaga is a demon, these folk thought singing the national anthem made you a demon. They had gigantic signs with religious slogans written on them standing out front of their own homes. I'll always remember one of those billboard signs that said something about the apocalypse, implying the end of the world was imminent. It was painted with a border design to make it appear as though the billboard itself was a page from the bible.

These people were weirdos to say the least. Unfortunately for me, they were just the type of weirdos that my parents felt should be brought into my life and have more influence over my identity than I myself was permitted to enjoy. I'll never understand my parents' logic if ever there was any logic behind it at all. One minute these people were just angry Amish folk with buttons on everything. In the next moment my mother had signed away all of my proverbial rights to this outlandish cult who just so happened to operate a youth group for kids about my age. Wouldn't you know. Wasn't that just simply spectacular that a cult was drawn toward a child like me, with parents like mine.

I am of course referring to them as a cult with derision and animosity. I'm sure that they don't view themselves as a cult. I'm sure that from their perspective, they're just a group of people who refuse to use deodorant and who think polyester and nylon are the evil work of Satan and one day through no fault of their own they saw an opportunity to try to indoctrinate me. Yeah, I'm sure that in their version of events I am some hell-ish child who wanted to wear boy underwear and t-shirts. I simply don't know why my attitude toward life as a child was deemed to be incorrect. Though, I now know that it was.

My parents delivered me into the waiting arms of this extremist religious group. I don't know how to describe how that felt as a young child. I was already socially othered and kept apart from my peers because my parents wouldn't allow me to wear any kind of comparable or similar clothing. I wasn't allowed to be like my peers, which was challenging enough for me. Now I was being sent to a hardcore, ultra right-wing religious group. Part of me wants to explain it through the lens of my trauma as an ominous place with warning signs emanating from the walls. My memory of that place where the cultish zealots met is so dark. I remember the darkness more than anything. It was literally dark there. I am not simply saying that to create an image. I guess standing on the side of a highway holding a sign that says "Jesus is disappointed in you" doesn't pay very well. So the place was literally dark because they weren't big on using electricity in this cult. For me, this was a dark and evil place both literally and figuratively. Though, that's partly my trauma talking. It was just a community hall. Just a building with a roof, walls, and a basement. It's around the corner from one of my favorite pizza places. It's a block away from a commercial district. There are old houses surrounding it. It was just a structure. A structure that still stands to this day.

I was sent down into that basement of that community hall. That's where the youth group service was held. I can feel my own mind resisting me as I try to remember the specifics. It's difficult and uncomfortable for me to pull these memories to the surface. I do it to tell my story though. I know that I have to tell my story in order to heal. That 'gospel hall' basement is one of the creepiest, most evil places I can imagine. Absolutely nothing good happened in that place. That gospel hall basement may as well have been a meeting point just outside the gates of hell.

I didn't have any kind of a choice. Nobody was ever going to listen to me or allow me to have my own kind of childhood. I think there was almost a hint of a sadistic enjoyment in sending me to that cult's youth group. Certainly it was known that I didn't want to go there and I didn't want to be a part of that horrible religious group. None of that mattered, though, not to my parents.

Down in that basement there were probably two dozen kids. I don't remember arriving or entering the hall. I only remember how creepy it was and that I was sitting alone that first night. I didn't have a friend in the world there. I wouldn't have wanted to make a friend there, either. It isn't a far stretch to say that this was like being brought into the middle of an Amish community breakfast and simply abandoned there. Everyone around you is remarkably different from you in every way, they are not interested in you, while all you would rather do is return to the modern world rather than remain with this group. And on top of it all there are no introductions or pleasantries which might make you feel even the slightest bit welcome.

Nope. I was just dropped off in a creepy community hall run by backward Amish-but-mean religious zealots and to top it all off there wasn't even a slight *welcome to the cult*. I just had to awkwardly become one of the crowd of children who made their way to the basement. My clothes made me stand out in the crowd for being a decade out of date. Which was far too modern for these backwoods weirdos who thought zippers were a trick from the Devil. Because, yeah, the Devil has been working this whole time on trying to trick you into using a zipper instead of buttons. Yup. That's what good versus evil is all about. Zippers.

That gospel hall basement was the creepiest place I've ever been. Even though I was a child I could feel it in the air. This wasn't the right place for me. Something was wrong. I knew it. I simply didn't have any way to escape. Even if I had gotten up and ran out of that creepy basement, I had nowhere to go. My parents had left me there. I had to wait for them to return and collect me. If I had misbehaved even in the slightest, I knew that I would pay a hefty physical toll for that when I got home.

I was trapped there. I was isolated, friendless, and scared. It was a creepy place to be and I was surrounded by creepy, completely dissimilar types of children. I hated it there. I wanted to leave from the moment I arrived. I was totally and completely uncomfortable and anxious. All of that was even before the old preacher had revealed himself.

Every cult has a leader. This particular cult was no different. It's just that this cult had an emphasis toward children, rather than weak-minded adults. I sat in my chair in that basement just hoping the time would expire in short order. I just needed to leave. I just wanted to be left alone. That isn't how any of it unfolded, unfortunately.

The preacher walked out from a side room in that basement. He stomped like a wrestler toward the theatrical ring. I watched uncomfortably as the preacher came into the room and stood at the front of the assembled rows of uncomfortable church chairs. He was old. I remember thinking how old he was. He was probably in his fifties which made him ancient to a 7 year old. He was old, cranky, and bombastic. He also happened to be about six foot three inches in height which meant that he towered over the young children who formed his captive audience. This man stood in front of a basement filled with little kids and he began lecturing us on the rules and commandments of Almighty God.

Unfortunately for me, I was sent to this cultish youth group more than just once. I was sent there continuously and despite my many objections. I complained that the chairs were uncomfortable. It wasn't any fun. I didn't like having to dress up in old-fashioned church clothing and sit like a stone statue amidst all these other kids who seemed to be far more engaged. They were all siblings, cousins, or tightly connected close associates of this religious sect. I was an outsider in every possible sense. I didn't like it there and I would have given anything to be able to go and participate in some of the normal childhood activities that other kids got to do.

What I wanted didn't matter. The more I protested the youth group the more convinced my mother became that I needed to be there and had something to gain from listening to the Old Testament.

That youth group congregated on Friday nights. It was every Friday night for months, perhaps more. There in that dark, uncomfortable basement I listened to this old angry preacher shout his message at the children – at me. Most of those kids were members of his own family. His own children, nieces, nephews, and extended relatives. Which I'm sure made him less frightening to those other kids, having some familiar connection to the bombastic preacher of doom. I was uniquely terrified amongst this wayward and misguided group. Their religious perspective was neither popular nor positive. It had no appeal. Every child in that basement was there by a matter of push rather than a matter of pull.

There were no other adults there. Nobody sat at the back and listened. There was no counter point of view. It was just him. Just that old, angry preacher and his desire to warp the minds of children. He told us that the Bible, including the Old Testament, was the *literal* word of Almighty God. This was different from the usual teachings I received on Sundays in church with my family with dozens of other adults in the pews. In my regular church services there was a heavy emphasis on the New Testament – the teachings of Jesus Christ. Jesus who healed, forgave, cleansed, and enlightened.

This was different. This was not about love. It was about hatred. It was not about enjoying life. It was about strict adherence to unbendable ancient doctrine.

"Vengeance shall be mine, God said!" the old preacher shouted with palpable anger in his heart.

There was no way to exit. I had no other choice. I was simply forced to listen to a hateful message that God will cast fire, brimstone, and plague upon anyone who commits a minor infraction. The Old Testament tells of a God who would command a father to murder his own son. Who would sink fishing vessels at whim. Who would flood the world in a planetary genocide as a corrective action for *his own* mistake. A God who would destroy a city and everyone in it if the residents were wholly homosexuals.

That God of the Old Testament seemed as angry, brutish, and objectionable as the old man standing before me demanding obedience. It was a difficult message to hear as a child who had been raised from birth to entirely and fully believe and accept that there *is* a God. There *is* a God and that God *is* what the preacher's say. Without question. Without doubt.

So these youth group lectures continued. I wouldn't be able to accurately recount how many times I was there. It has been too long and this is something I never wanted to remember. I buried as many of these details as I could. I know that I was forced to attend this cultish youth group for at least a few months. How many months? I honestly don't know. Long enough to become psychologically scarred. One night in particular impacted me more than all of the others.

It had all been building toward something. A big 'final lesson' was a part of the preacher's plan.

Then one night that message was delivered in a stern, prosecutorial gaze. The lecture that night crushed my heart and soul. This man was an authoritarian. He was angry. This was a man with violence in his soul. I could sense it. I could feel it emanating from him. Even at that age I could sense danger from an angry adult. A lesson I'd learned at the literal hands of my own father. I knew when I was facing a man whose moral compass allowed for brutality against a defenseless child.

This man was a brute.

He stood wearing a wool suit. I remember that because it set him apart from regular society. These religious extremists stood out in a crowd. You could compare one of them against someone who was just a normal properly-hinged everyday person. I'll never forget that preacher. I will never forget how unpleasant it was to sit in that basement and listen to his rants. This was not a man preaching love, forgiveness, acceptance, and peace. No. This was a man preaching fire, brimstone, pestilence, vengeance, and judgment.

This man was preaching *hatred*. Worse: he was *programming* hatred. If you hated who he told you to hate then you would receive the bounty of heaven and everlasting life. If you abided by the doctrine which he shouted had come straight from the word of God Almighty then you would be 'first in line' to receive God's rewards. Do as I say. Think what I tell you to think. Abide by the values and restrictions that I shall dictate and you will be spared an eternity of being burned alive by goat-faced slithering monsters.

I was able to withstand all of that. Up until that point. I handled it. I sat there and I received the message of God, as it was being presented to me. But it was about to go further than my mind as a lonely child could process.

"I changed the oil in my truck this afternoon," he said with an angry glare emanating from his stony-face.

"This is the rag that I used to clean up the oil!" The preacher raised his hand high into the air as he presented an oil-stained rag. I looked at the rag in his hand as he dangled it, slowly scanning the room making eye contact with each of the frightened children. He was intimidating. After all, he was a tall and angry brute. But he was also speaking in the name of Almighty God. The creator. The holy spirit. The preacher was delivering *God's own* message. A message which I at least found terrifying.

"This is what God sees when he looks at *you*," the preacher said, still dangling the dirty rag.

"God sees a filthy rag. That's what you are: a filthy rag. You were born covered in the stains of sin. You are filthy! Filthy! Disgusting sinners! Only God can wash away the stains from your soul and allow you into heaven!" the preacher shouted.

You could feel the fear and the tension as frightened children nervously peered upward at the angry preacher. He went on with his colorful metaphor for several more minutes. A young girl raised her hand to ask a question. He called on her and allowed her to speak.

"What does God want us to do to get into heaven?" she asked.

The preacher began explaining the perfection of heaven and how only the children of God will be permitted to enter heaven when they die. There are few spaces in heaven, he said. Only the 'cleanest' of God's children will earn entry into

the afterlife. He continued to explain how we are born
sinners and must be cleansed. Only Jesus Christ can cleanse
us, he said. Either you accept Jesus Christ into your heart
and soul and acknowledge him as your lord and savior or you
will be condemned to the fire pits of hell for all eternity.

I was truly scared. I think we were all scared. We had all
been primed in the prior weeks to have a deep fear of both
hell and God's wrath. It was a scary thing for a child to hear,
especially to have it shouted at you by a lunatic holding an
oily rag in your face. Still it got worse.

I sat there feeling intimidated and uncomfortable. I didn't
want there to be a place so horrible as hell. I certainly didn't
want such a terrible place to be a potential destination on
any path that I may walk. It didn't seem fair to me. It didn't
seem right. Yet, I had been taught my entire life that God is
real. Heaven is real. Hell is real. The Bible is the literal word
of God and the ministers and preachers are unassailable
heralds and witnesses to his word.

Then it happened. I don't remember the exact words. It's
been too long and I've run from this memory my entire life
but I remember exactly the essence of the message which the
preacher conveyed that night. It went into my ears, straight

through my brain and became entrenched in my guts like tumors. That angry preacher, speaking in the name of God, my ultimate judge who singularly determines my eternal fate, declared that those oily stains of sin can only be washed away by Jesus Christ – and that some sins *can never be cleansed.* There are *unforgivable sins* which immediately, irrevocably condemn any person to hell for all eternity.

Then he gave an example: homosexual sex.

God. *Hates.* Fags.

Hearing that message from a preacher of God forever altered my trajectory in life. It was a shattering shock to my system. I was terribly, truly afraid.

As I sit in the tranquility of my own home now almost thirty years later I have tears streaming down my face. I don't know when I figured it out. I don't know how I learned about sex or more specifically homosexual sex. At that moment, though, I did know. I had done that. I was one of the people the preacher was talking about. I am the oil stain that can never be cleansed. The sin that can never be forgiven. I am unworthy of God's love. *Forever.* I am condemned to hell for eternity.

From that moment on my life held no meaning nor value. I was a filthy, oil-stained, cursed, homosexual sinner.

I sit sobbing now in the present because it hurts me now as powerfully as it hurt me then. I was a child. I was just a young, lonely child.

I was filled with absolute fear. I felt that fear run through my body, my heart, my soul. I was stunned. Shocked. Mortified. How can God condemn me for all eternity over a game in the woods? A game I never understood? A childhood error. What kind of God is that heartless, cruel, unfair, and unjust?

I did the only thing that I could do. I tried to inoculate myself as best as I could. Out of absolute horror and fear, I sat in that basement and silently prayed to Jesus Christ to come into my heart and become my lord and savior. Not out of love. Not out of happiness. Not out of inner peace. Not out of thoughtful desire.

It was out of unmitigated terror and in total duress that I summoned Jesus Christ to save me and to wash away my sins. All of them.

I was deathly frightened, believing the devil and evil demon spirits were lurking in the shadows waiting to drag me to the depths of hell.

I left the youth group that night in a trance. As we left the basement one-by-one the preacher handed each of us a Skor bar. That was the end of the youth group. He'd caused me so much harm and all that I got in return was, literally, a Skor bar. Who the hell eats a Skor bar?

I don't know if I ever attended the youth group after that night. My memories are so faded that I simply can't be certain. While it's possible that was my last night in the youth group, I can state unequivocally that this was the beginning of a lifetime of sadness, pain, emotional instability, and hiding parts of myself. The virus had now been implanted into my thoughts. It was there now, backed up by God himself.

Chapter 3
A Secret Never to be Known

I had a secret that no other person could ever know. I had the weight of heaven and hell on my shoulders. I was a marked child. I was cursed. The only thing that I could do is keep my secret and plead for forgiveness. With enough pleading, perhaps God would show mercy. I didn't know how to plead. Or when or where one even could without drawing the attention of family. I had to delay my inevitable pleading. I had to wait until the time was right. Until then, the very thought of any of this was entirely unbearable. I took my sins and my childhood sexual experience and I shoved them all down into the darkness. Down and out of my mind. I couldn't handle even a brief recollection. Those memories were all so overwhelming.

At a very young age I decided that having friends leads to pain. Friends are the people who cause you to unwittingly become condemned. Who needed friends, then? On the one hand, my parents would sabotage any possibility I might have to develop friendships or connections with other people. On the other hand, I was pretty good at sabotaging friendships all on my own with the behavioral oddities I was developing as I tried to work through my own dilemma. Throughout my early school years I was always noticeably different from the other kids. Everyone else wore brand name clothes that they likely picked themselves. I wore ill-fitted clothing, which was never a name brand. Others were encouraged to dream, be creative, and imagine an exciting future. I was encouraged to be silent. Silent is exactly what I became. Silent, different, and a loner. Which in itself then became a cause for concern which made people want to inquire.

I don't quite remember the sequence of events which led to my unfortunate reintroduction to that old preacher. I guess it was because there was something noticeably wrong with me. I wasn't fitting in. I wasn't happy. Which meant that someone would inevitably come to ask what was wrong. Unfortunately for me, that person was the old preacher. The last person on earth I wanted to speak with or spend any time alone with was the preacher.

I had to endure several one-on-one sessions with the preacher. Those memories are dark and blurry, encapsulated in stress. At this stage of my life I have truly tried to remember what led to these events. I simply cannot fully recall. I know that there was some sort of suspicion toward me. I know that it began, innocently enough, from my math homework. Something I said or something I did with my math homework landed me back face-to-face with the preacher. The fact that I had become an obviously unhappy loner only added to the suspicions.

These memories are cloudy and hazy from my fear, stress, and discomfort. I was never comfortable with the preacher to say the least. I distinctly remember being brought back to that horrible, dark 'gospel hall.' I sat across a small table from the old preacher who simply stared at me. He stared without speaking. I'll never forget how uncomfortable I was as a young child to be sitting there in that small room with an old man just glaring into me. There was never anyone else around, either. Nobody in the next room or anywhere in the building at all. I was just alone with this old man, glaring into me with painfully uncomfortable silence.

I don't remember him ever saying anything in those sessions. Not even a word. He simply stared at me. He just stared into my eyes and kept angrily awaiting something. I remember thinking that he wanted me to confess something. I was afraid. I was always afraid. I didn't have any words to say. I was trapped, alone, and scared. I knew that this old man wanted something from me. I knew that he shouldn't. I knew that it was wrong. I was so scared. A child cannot defend themselves against a full-grown adult. A trapped child can do even less when faced with a perceived authority figure.

The preacher had power. The preacher had strength, buttressed by a palpable anger that I could feel emanating from him. I was alone, terrified, and powerless. I was a small child who nobody of any relevance wanted to listen to. Nobody protected me. Nobody rescued me. I felt as though I was constantly being placed in a position of danger. Danger from other people. Other people were dangerous to me, and to my secret. I was there, alone, to be interrogated and corrected by the old preacher. Whatever it was that someone felt needed to be corrected in me, I suppose I'll never know. Or perhaps I'll never admit it even to myself.

It's very difficult for me to share that story, as vague as my recollection may be. These memories are buried beneath layer after layer of psychological shielding. I had to bury these memories to survive. I had to forget and erase it all in order to move forward. My childhood trauma scarred me so deeply that my mind had to create ways to heal itself from my own experiences. It wasn't long before my trauma began to manifest in other ways.

I developed body-image issues in junior high. I felt very uncomfortable with my appearance all of the time. I also became terrified with the thought of anyone coming near my penis. I never wanted anyone to touch, or come close to touching, my penis. I didn't want to be touched. I never wanted to allow anyone to touch me. I began wearing shorts between my underwear and my pants. Even in the summer, I wore multiple layers no matter how hot it was. I needed barriers to protect me. Then I started wearing three t-shirts layered on top of one another. I was rapidly developing an anxiety disorder, though nobody seemed to notice. At least nobody offered any guidance or help.

It wasn't long after I began wearing multiple layers of clothing that I began 'cutting.' I don't know how it started. Just one day I began cutting myself with a razor blade. Then with knives. I would cut my legs and arms where nobody would see and then cover myself in layers of clothing. I still have scars on my body from those teenage years. I would cut myself just to feel the physical pain. I would feel that pain and process it. I could look at the blade and the blood and understand that I am hurt. I could understand why. That was a pain my mind was able to handle.

I was cutting and I was angry. I had been taught that God hated gay people. My biggest ambition in life – my only ambition in life – was to win God's approval for my existence. Since God hated the gays, so did I. That hatred took root and began rapidly growing within me. Hatred can grow ever so quickly within the heart of a hurting, wounded person, I learned. That was certainly my experience. Hatred, anger, and violent desires became my everything. All that I was.

I knew that I was angry. I knew that something was wrong. I didn't know what it was, though. Whether or not 'memory repression' is a scientifically valid concept I can say with high certainty that in my lived experience I did in fact repress memories of my same-sex encounter for many years. I repressed the memory and I accepted new lines of thinking. I was in a form of survival mode. I had to become something else in order to protect myself. I became a person who didn't have those experiences or memories. I was a person who embraced the religious beliefs which had been forced on me. I would never dare to use the lord's name in vain. I would never deny believing in Jesus Christ. There were lines in the sand which became sacred to me. All of them were essentially core beliefs of an ultra-conservative form of Christianity.

It wasn't that I had drank the Kool-Aid. It was that I firmly believed that I needed to behave as if I had drank the Kool-Aid.

I might have been the only teenager at the time who held strongly oppositional views toward gay marriage. Which is beyond peculiar as I shouldn't have had any reason whatsoever to hold an opinion of any nature on that topic. It didn't matter though. I needed to win God's forgiveness. I needed to hate who God hates and I needed to punish myself so that God would not need to punish me with banishment to hell.

I became a skilled professional at punishing myself. I didn't make friends. I didn't have fun. I didn't live my life. I hated. I hurt. I cut. I cried alone in the dark.

I started experiencing suicidal ideation in junior high. I was a loner. My parents took every opportunity to ensure that I was separated from the herd. In eighth grade I was the only student in my school whose parents declined consent for me to participate in Sex Education. The teachers didn't make it any easier for me either when they made a rather public display of pulling me out of the classroom prior to each Sex Ed lesson. It was humiliating. Of course I was starting to fantasize of suicide. I didn't have a reason to live. Life itself was misery. Still, I wasn't able to remember what had happened. I was completely miserable but I didn't know why.

I always knew that something was wrong. My family also knew that something was wrong. They chose to deal with that by openly musing that they felt I would ultimately grow up to become a serial killer. I wish I could say this was a cruel joke. Sadly, it's true. My two eldest brothers on numerous occasions said both to me directly and to others in my presence that they felt I was exhibiting early warning signs of becoming a serial killer.

Their assessment was rather flimsy, not that it made the comments sting any less. According to them, when I was very young I tried to feed chocolate chips to a stray kitten I'd taken home after finding it in a field. They called this "torturing animals." Then they said that I hated gay people, which must be a sign that I'd develop into a homicidal maniac targeting the gay community. My eldest brother even went so far as to say he discussed the matter with his friend who was an expert in psychology and she agreed that I was exhibiting troubling signs of one day becoming a serial killer. That so-called expert in psychology completed Psych 101 before dropping out to become a part-time gas station attendant.

You would think that any parent would protect their child from the psychological abuse of being told they will one day become a serial killer. In my case, my mother reacted as though this was a concerning possibility worthy of further discourse. Whatever may have been intended on their part the end result was that I felt very deeply flawed. I felt that I was both unloved and unlovable. God hated me. Why wouldn't my own family hate me, too?

Something that always lingers in my mind when I think back to those days that I will never understand is that I was the only kid in school who didn't get lunch. My parents just didn't give me either food or money to buy food. I will never understand why. No matter how hard-up they may have been financially they still could have been able to provide me with lunch. They weren't poor. In fact, they were the second-largest financial contributors to our church. They could have fed their own child, and if preparing a lunch had been inconvenient they certainly could have given me cash to eat at the cafeteria. How could such strict members of the Christian faith consciously decide not to feed one of their own children? Everyone else was fed every meal. Just not me. They simply couldn't be bothered to do it. I was an invisible, unloved ghost-child.

So I cut myself some more. Then I learned to avoid others and to be alone as much as possible. My home didn't feel like a psychologically safe place for me. Every night I would leave and walk the streets alone. I was alone with nothing but my music. As my pain increasingly turned to anger, my anger increasingly pushed me toward more aggressive kinds of music. I became a huge fan of Eminem. Eminem, as most would recall from that era, was no friend of the gay community. He produced violent songs which blatantly supported and fostered homophobia. To say nothing of the song "Kim" in which he portrays the murder of his own wife.

I spent hours walking the streets listening to that form of aggressive, violent, destructive content.

By the time I got to high school I was suffering from severe anxiety and depression. I made a few friends in high school. Not many, but I wasn't completely alone anymore. I drifted away from my family and wanted to branch out and attempt to be social. But I didn't know how. My social skills were years behind those of my peers. Everyone else seemed to be finding themselves and learning new things and becoming unique individuals. I still had no identity. If I had any kind of an identity at all, it was merely a cheap replication of Eminem. Which was hardly a persona worthy of impersonation.

I was 15 years old when I first began to suffer from insomnia. I had my first job, working part-time at a coffee shop. As an adult I now realize that the wealthy restaurateur who owned that shop was enriching himself by hurting teenage kids. They had us working from the minute we got out of school sometimes until 2:00am. For a time they wouldn't even tell us when our shift would end, they'd just say we would be there until they would let us leave. That could be anywhere between 10:00pm and 2:00pm. On school nights. Night after night.

Some parents stepped in and contacted the labor department. The coffee shop stopped giving shifts to the staff whose parents wouldn't tolerate those abuses. My parents never said a word. So I kept working. There was no time for homework and no time for sleep. They would even switch to having the high school-aged staff working evenings to working all day on Saturdays. So you might work until 11:00pm on a Friday and have to be up and back at work for 7:00am on Saturday. As a high school student. It was the Saturday morning shifts that gave me insomnia. I couldn't regulate my sleep and I found myself just worrying that I wasn't falling asleep on time. I worried that I couldn't fall asleep and I worried that I'd sleep too late in the morning and get into trouble.

So I'd just worry. All night.

That's when I started taking sleeping pills. It's also when I first developed an awareness that something wasn't right with my mental health. I began pushing my parents to take me to the doctor, hoping the doctor would take one look at me and figure out my mental health issues. If only mental health issues were as apparent as broken bones that might have worked. The doctor didn't see anything wrong with me. He just thought I was some overly shy kid.

I kept going to the doctor while I was in high school. Something was wrong with me and I needed help. I wasn't able to articulate what was wrong. I simply kept presenting to the doctor's office waiting for them to spontaneously decipher my inner pain and set about curing me. Inevitably the doctors decided I was depressed and prescribed me an antidepressant.

I loathe antidepressants. For whatever reason, I have such a strong aversion to an antidepressant that I absolutely will not take one for longer than a week or two. I've been prescribed antidepressants probably 12-15 times in my life. Which is to say, I've been on antidepressants for maybe a few months of my life.

Following this stint in the psych ward I was prescribed Paxil. Unlike Effexor, Paxil didn't cause headaches or confusion. In fact it only did two things: it made me exhausted and it deprived me of the ability to have an orgasm. One night when I would have been about 18 I was having sex with my beautiful girlfriend at the time on a couch outside her older sister's bedroom. I kept thrusting away as vigorously as I could for well over an hour before giving up. I couldn't cum. No matter how hard I tried, Paxil wouldn't let me have an orgasm. After I finally gave up and we put our clothes back on, my girlfriend's sister who would have been 22 at the time, came out of her bedroom. She gave a very impatient glare to my girlfriend, looked at me and began to blush before darting off without saying a word. We thought she was already gone for the night. It turns out we had started getting frisky right as she had been about to come out of her bedroom. She froze and stood silent at the door for over an hour unsure of what to do.

That was the end of Paxil.

Still, in high school it was obvious that something was wrong. I began to show physical symptoms. My stomach was always upset. Obviously in my teen years I had poor eating habits. I had limited ability to prepare my own food and my parents seemed to firmly believe that preparing one meal per day at dinner was sufficient. My stomach issues were more than that though. My stomach and my gut were always very easily unsettled. Then I started having worse issues.

One morning I woke to find a pool of blood had flowed out of my penis. It was everywhere in my bed and on my clothes. I was embarrassed and covered up the evidence as best I could. A short while later it happened again. Then one morning when I went to urinate a steady stream of blood flowed out of me. This went on for months. One time when I thought I needed to urinate I expelled a significant quantity of blood. So much that I knew I was in serious trouble and I couldn't keep hiding it.

I went to the doctor and so began a very difficult chapter in my youth. There was talk that I may be suffering from bladder cancer. I needed surgery. But all I was hearing was that I was going to need to expose my penis to other people. To men. Men who were going to need to touch it. I tried to express my hesitancy and lack of comfort with what the doctors were telling me. At the time I was in an examination room with two male doctors.

One of them looked at me and said "It's like you're going to tell us that you have three balls or something. C'mon, we've seen it all before."

Around this time I made my first suicide attempt. I overdosed on that bottle of antidepressants I'd previously left untouched. I'd rather die than have a man fondle my penis, even if he was a doctor.

I spent a week in the psychiatric ward of the hospital. In the psych ward they rolled out some catholic supremacist nut-job. He wasn't a psychiatrist or a psychologist. He may have been a social worker. Whatever he was, he was neither qualified nor helpful. He accused me of faking a suicide attempt for attention and said that I must have Histrionic Personality Disorder. Then after accusing me of being a fraud, he fought to have me held in the psych ward for a full month.

Because if you think I'm faking a mental health condition, the appropriate response is to reward that fakery with a month of unnecessary treatments? I'm not quite sure what his logical process was on that one. All that I know for sure is that he didn't want to understand or to help. He wanted to be the one who decides and dishes out discipline. Typical religious twit.

Years later I saw him on the local news bemoaning the diminished state of the catholic church in society. So sad to see the papists witnessing the erosion of their imperial bank which masquerades as a church. Every time I learn of the reduction of the little catholic empire, I think of this small man K.M. and I take some satisfaction from knowing that organization has been lessened and rightfully diminished.

I returned to school after my brief stint in the hospital. I was less comfortable than ever. After all, I'd been told I'm nothing but a dramatic whiner seeking attention with no legitimate issues in life. The school wasn't quite sure what was going on with me but they were willing to let me ease back into regular teenage life. I remember there was an exam coming up in my accounting class, which the school offered to delay until I was feeling better. It was a minor, though appreciated, accommodation for a teenager still unsure of whether he has cancer and whose thoughts were often of suicide and self-harm.

When my mother found out that I had received some "special treatment" because of my ongoing medical status she was furious. The thought of anyone accommodating me after I had been such a nuisance as to end up in the hospital was too much for my mother. So she called the school and told them I had been lying. About everything. She said I made up the cancer scare entirely and had never even been to the doctor.

My own mother did this to me.

The school administrators were absolutely furious. They flunked me. They treated me as if I had simply been AWOL for exams. All of my friends – the very few that I had – got to graduate high school and move on with their lives. But not me.

I had to do an extra semester in high school to earn those credits. Alone. Completely alone.

It's been over 15 years and my mother has never apologized or even remotely admitted that what she did was cruel or even wrong. She says she doesn't remember me ever having a medical issue. How very Christian of her – convenient lies and cruelty. Very Christian indeed.

Chapter 4
Self-Medicating into Numbness

In my early twenties I began having strange thoughts. A memory would begin to rise to the surface. A memory of the woods with those boys. Whenever the memory would start to bubble up my thoughts would go haywire, my stomach would churn, and I would begin to sweat. I would have a panic attack. The memory would slip away. This kept happening to me over and over. The memory trying to rise to the surface followed by the intense psychological and physiological response.

Around the same time I began drinking alcohol. I'd never been around anyone who drank. My parents have never tasted alcohol. I didn't know how to drink at first but I quickly learned. Alcohol was like a magical cure for all of my problems. I wasn't anxious. I was social. People seemed to find me funny and amusing. I even made numerous new friendships. It was the biggest social circle I've ever had in my life. I had a strong group of friends. We drank, we partied, we fucked like rabbits, and in a way I was finally free. I was someone. I was a person with a clothing style, music that I liked, foods that I liked, restaurants that I liked, girls who I liked. I was forming an identity for the first time in my life that was distinctly and truly my own.

I loved alcohol. Years of insomnia were suddenly ended by passing out. Years of social ineptitude were behind me. When I was drunk I could talk to anyone, even the prettiest girl in the room. When I was drinking the pretty girls seemed to like me. It was glorious and wonderful. I was having the time of my life.

I always thought that I was drinking because of my social anxiety. I feel very nervous in social settings, particularly with new people. I've always struggled to feel like I fit in. My mind works differently than everyone else's. I get nervous, then anxious, then I start sweating, and then I feel a sharp pain in my gut whenever I step into a social encounter. Things like job interviews or first dates are torture for me. Alcohol became my only coping mechanism for social settings. Though, that obviously doesn't work for every situation. Which led me to eliminate any scenario in which alcohol couldn't play a role.

Except for thoughts and feelings and memories I couldn't understand. They kept coming back. My emotions were becoming more difficult to control. I was negative, cranky, and could become a bull of toxic rage in an instant. I had so much anger inside that I couldn't contain it. I couldn't control it. It was coming out on its own more and more. I began to realize that I was hiding things, even from myself. The memory bubbled up to the surface so many times that I couldn't ignore it anymore. I knew it was there. I knew it was harming me. Somehow this memory and the way I had to suppress it was causing me intense psychological duress.

I allowed myself to think about it. To remember bits and pieces. I would sit alone in the dark and I would drink. I would drink and let the memory come forward, little pieces at a time. Invariably, I would become overwhelmed with sadness, sorrow, and shame. I would break down sobbing before pleading with God to forgive me. The sorrow that I feel in my heart and soul is the most powerful emotion I have ever experienced. It is stronger than any feeling of love or affection. It is stronger than any feeling of happiness, pride, achievement, or relief.

The strongest emotion that I have is *sorrow*.

Not long ago Spotify randomly played a song 'A jar of hearts' by Christina Perri. She sings the lyrics *"I learned to live half alive..."* with such hearty sincerity. Those words instantly resonated with me and I played the song over and over. It may have been her singing but those were my scars and my reality I was singing along to. I did learn to live half alive. From 5:00pm onward I was a dysfunctional disaster. My house was unclean and in disarray. I didn't spend money on nice clothes, furniture, or decorations. It was just me and alcohol. Alone together.

Night after night. Month after month. The years passed me by. I was growing more and more miserable. In my misery I turned more and more to the booze.

I won't say that I became 'an alcoholic' because that is an out-dated and needlessly stigmatizing term. I did, however, become a person diagnosed with 'alcohol use disorder.' I drank every day for over 15 years. Not just a few drinks, either. I drank myself to a stupor every night for over 15 years. During that time I made terrible life choices. I hurt people. I lied about myself. I lied about others. I lied to hide my drinking. And I totally lost control of my life, my emotions, my finances, and my grip on reality.

I had no identity except for the shallow falsehoods I held up as shields to protect myself. I didn't want anyone to get close. I didn't want them to see too much or figure things out. What if I said more than I should? What if I accidentally revealed more of myself than I intended to? When you live with a terrible secret so powerful that you can't allow even yourself to know what that secret is, friendships and relationships are perceived as threatening liabilities to be avoided.

I went through life drinking, lying, pretending to be something I'm not. I had no direction nor real ambition. I was adrift. Lost. I had no anchor to anything. I wasn't rooted in family, in faith, in personal principle, nor a driving determination. All that I had was alcohol. Alcohol that made me feel more comfortable and numb. As a person running from a memory, alcohol proved to be a great addition to daily life. My memory worsened. My emotions seemed less sharp. For whatever reason, life seemed almost tolerable despite being completely pointless.

Believe it or not I actually went to university and graduated with a degree. Though it was not without its challenges. I was a person who had an obvious chip on his shoulder. I didn't socialize or make many friends. I was someone who everyone else loved to hate. Because I'm so listless and confused by my own identity I found myself constantly trying to present false versions of who I wished I could be. Most people picked up on that rather quickly and many of them weren't shy to express their dislike of me as a person. Even some of my professors seemed to gleefully advertise their disapproval of my worldview.

I met a girl in university who seemed to have a kind heart with a mysterious fun side to her. I was still trying to figure myself out. I was still trying to win the affection of my parents and my family. Most of all, I was still trying to win the forgiveness of God for my childhood sexual encounter. So I pursued the cute super-religious girl I met on campus. She was ultra religious, in fact. She checked off all of the boxes my parents would be looking for if they got to choose my wife.

Even in my early twenties when everyone else was having random sex with people they'd just bumped into in the hallway, I was just looking for a fake relationship with a Christian girl who'd camouflage my past and appease those around me. She wasn't what I wanted. She was what others hoped I would want.

Her name was Lisa. A thin blonde who always wore skirts. We met at a party where everyone was drinking and I felt right at home. In those days Facebook had just come out like last Tuesday and it was actually a wonderful website then. It hadn't become evil yet and it wasn't a place where every corporation, politician, and government agency was trying to invade your life. People didn't even tinker with their privacy settings. It was just horny university students looking to find people to, shall we say, connect.

Which is how Lisa and I connected after the party. We couldn't go home together that night because, well, Lisa had a boyfriend. As horny girls that age did in those situations, she needed to run home and delete the evidence of her boyfriend before I could see it. She was hiding the fact that she had a boyfriend while I was hiding the fact that I was very damaged as a person. We spent weeks talking to each other over Facebook, both of us lying about certain things. I don't remember when I found out that she had a boyfriend that she was hiding from me, but I remember that I didn't much care. In a strange way, I liked it that she had a boyfriend. Maybe it was the chip on my shoulder or maybe my self-esteem was just so depleted that I needed to 'beat' someone in a contest to sleep with her. I don't know what it was. Pursuing women who already have significant others became my trademark for a time.

One night Lisa was telling me about her faith in God. I know. That's very peculiar. A twenty-year-old girl initiates an emotional affair behind her boyfriend's back, while proclaiming her supreme religiosity. Young people make curious decisions. It didn't matter. We had an attraction and we were both seeking to act upon it, contradictions be damned.

Lisa told me she has a strong, powerful connection with God. She could feel God's presence in her life. Of course, I was more than intrigued. Deep down all I ever wanted was to feel God's presence and to have his forgiveness. Now I have a pretty girl cock-teasing me while telling me she also brings the holy spirit along with her? Sign me up.

She kept talking to me about her faith. She told me the energy that she feels when God embraces her. I wasn't rolling my eyes or mocking her. I believed her. I was fully primed to believe her. Then something happened which was unlike any experience I've ever had before. I also felt God's presence. It was a surreal experience. The hair on my body felt electrified as I suddenly felt that God was there with me. Not only was he with me but Lisa suddenly felt his presence as well. If you've never had an experience such as this it probably sounds fake, exaggerated, or ridiculous. I can say with full clarity and confidence that I experienced something eye-opening that night.

I felt what I understood to be God.

It wasn't the God that angry old preacher lectured me about. It was a loving God. A God who didn't hate me. A God who wanted to share something with me.

At that moment, both Lisa and I understood that God was telling us something very important. Not that we were soulmates. Not that we were going to be together forever.

Not that this was meant to be. Actually, it was the opposite. God was telling us that we were going to be together for a time during which Lisa would endure an intense health-related challenge. We both felt it. We both understood it. In that moment, we both completely understood that we were about to walk a path together which would be exceedingly difficult but that we would both be stronger people when our paths diverged.

No, I wasn't on drugs. No, I wasn't drunk at the time.

I felt it. Nobody will ever be able to convince me that God wasn't at work with Lisa and I that night.

We both heard that message loud and clear and we both acted upon it. Though, admittedly, we did not go about things in the most honorable sequence. There were many things that I truly loved about Lisa. One of them was the fact that she kept telling me she was a virgin. She wasn't. But she somehow thought that she was and she loved telling me that I was going to be 'her first.' She wasn't lying. She really did somehow think I was going to be her first, despite the fact that her boyfriend in high school had on numerous occasions inserted his dick into her vagina.

Lisa felt that since he didn't move around very much that this didn't count as being sex. That was a logical train of thought that only a Catholic girl could have and it amused me to no end. Of course I just went along with it even as I was pushing myself inside her for *our* first time, pretending it was also *her* first time. Which of course it wasn't.

Regrettably, we didn't wait for her to actually end things with the boyfriend she'd attempted to hide from me for some weeks at that point. It makes me feel more honorable and decent to pretend that I feel badly about that fact. In reality, I developed a strong sense of excitement and exhilaration from sleeping with some other guy's girl. That is a detestable trait which unfortunately persisted within me for quite some time.

Lisa did then go and break up with her boyfriend. We then did what 20-something kids in university do: we had sex everywhere we physically could. The two of us were great together. Somehow we realized that we both had a kinky side. So not only were we having sex three times a day but we were also having all kinds of kinky sex. There were toys, handcuffs, whips, some rough spanking and aggression, and plenty more. I've never admitted this to anyone before but at one point in time that ultra-religious Catholic girl came back from the mall with a smile from ear-to-ear as she pulled a paper bag from her purse. She blushed like she really was a virgin as she pulled out a hot-pink, frilly thong. I looked at it totally confused. She wore small-size panties but the thong in her hands was definitely closer to size large.

I stared at her blankly and confused.

"You're going to wear it!" she squealed. "You're going to wear it and I am going to call you *my cuckold!*"

That's when I learned that she actually thoroughly enjoyed the fact that she had been cheating on her previous boyfriend with me. As it turns out, she was making sure that he knew little details all along. I don't fully know that side of the story, so I'll leave it at that.
We had an immense amount of kinky fun together. We tried every kind of role playing, used every toy, and we could turn anything into a kinky secret between us. Simply put, we had fun and we truly did love each other.

After we had been together for a little over a year it happened. Lisa was diagnosed with a life-threatening medical condition. I won't reveal what it was because that's her story (of course you know "Lisa" isn't her real name, anyway). Only she has the right to tell her own story.

What I can say is that we spent another year-and-a-half together while she was dealing with a medical condition. We both felt as though we were exactly where we were meant to be, with the person we were meant to be with, and she got through it. We had an intensely spiritual beginning and we both heard a supernatural message which came to fruition. That's how I know God is real. That's *one* of the experiences in my adult life where God made his presence – and his message – inescapably clear to me.

What has taken me far, far too long to fully appreciate is that I have had these experiences in feeling God's presence. It was a loving presence. A guiding presence. A powerful spirit who wished me no harm, who didn't hate me or view me as being a filthy rag. In those moments I was experiencing God's love. Yet the fear and the self-loathing and the worthlessness and the condemnation that I was programmed to feel from that preacher somehow took precedence and overrode even those experiences of actually feeling God's presence.

That's how entrenched the anti-gay messaging has been within my mind and body throughout my life.

After Lisa recovered and she was as fully healed as she could be from her medical issue we both seemed to intuitively know that our time on that path together had come to an end. We didn't fight. We didn't stop loving one another. We didn't cheat or betray. We just accepted that whatever intense spark had existed between us was no longer there. We hugged, kissed, let go of each others' hand and began walking our separate paths. Lisa moved shortly thereafter, heading east. It took me a while longer but I moved as well, headed west.

As I write these words I'm astonished to admit that Lisa and I never saw each other again. After all these years, all that we went through together, you'd think that we might have crossed paths again. Or at least that I might have noticed the fact that I never saw my first true love again. The memory of her and our time together was always enough.

We truly were brought together only for a short time. Even now I believe that with all my heart. It was a connection that was meant to be, and meant to end when it did.

Chapter 5
Broken Beyond Broke

After Lisa was gone I continued to drink frequently and heavily. I was spending much more money on alcohol than I could actually afford. Part of me knew that I was numbing the pain of my past. Another part of me realized how much more fun and socially accepted I found myself while drinking. There were many things pulling me toward alcohol. For me, at least in the beginning, it brought a range of benefits both therapeutic, medicinal, and personality-enhancing. Booze is expensive though, and I was nowhere near to being rich.

I'll never forget one night in the summer of 2009. It must have been June or July. I was laying in bed after having a few glasses of wine with friends. I could feel myself drinking off to sleep. Then I remembered the night before and how easily I'd fallen asleep, with the help of some wine that night too. It struck me at that moment that wine had relaxed me enough that I could just go to bed and drift off to sleep. I'd never been able to do that before. I felt almost giddy at the thought of it. Wine was an incredible discovery for me. It solved so many of the challenges I'd been facing. Those were my thoughts as I fell asleep that night. It was all burned into my memory.

My credit card balance was always increasing. I recognize now how unhelpful this was for me in the long-term but back then it seemed like my credit card provider was increasing my borrowing limit every few months. The more they allowed me to borrow, the more I spent on alcohol. I kept spending until I had credit card debt which was equal to 30% of my annual income at the time. That was just my credit card debt. I also had about $50,000 in student loan debt. That's a difficult hole to climb out from especially when your drinking is still completely out of control. I knew that I had money problems. Still, I wasn't prepared to admit that I had a drinking problem.

I don't know what triggered it but one day the credit card company said 'enough' and shut down my cards. No more borrowing. On top of that, they wanted to be paid back immediately. In full. That obviously wasn't going to happen. I wish that I had been able to see into the future and make the right decision at the time. Instead I did exactly the wrong thing. I kept making payments on my defaulted credit cards. Whatever I was in life I wasn't the kind of person who borrows money and doesn't pay it back. I had a sense of integrity. I was going to pay back the credit card debt. Or so I thought.

If I knew how it would all unfold I would have just accepted the inevitable and let the credit card company record the bad debts on my bureau reports. I should have. It would have been easier that way. The bad debts being recorded on my credit bureau files happened anyway. It was inevitable with my complete inability to manage my own finances.

Not understanding how those processes work, I continued to pay a few hundred dollars per month toward my credit card debts. I wasn't making a dent in the rapidly accumulating interest but what I was doing was keeping the debts fresh. Each payment kept the debt 'new' when what I really needed was for it to be 6 years old, and fall off my bureau reports.

I quickly learned that I couldn't afford to live, drink, and pay my debts. In fact, I could only comfortably afford one of the three. So I did what many people with drinking problems do when faced with that dilemma. I barely lived – and I drank.

If I could have opted just for the drinking, I likely would have done that. But I was fond of staying dry so I continued to try to pay rent. Though I didn't always pay the electric bill.

I was financially destitute. The lending agency was always chasing me to pay my student loans which, embarrassingly, I couldn't even process that line of thinking. "How do you think you're going to get blood from a stone?" I would bark at them with an attitude. I didn't have any money. I was poorer than not having any money. I had so much debt that creditors were lining up to compete for who was going to get the half-empty bottle of Frank's Red Hot sauce from my fridge.

Depression set in and the self-loathing became unbearable.

This wasn't supposed to happen to me. I'm a nice guy. I'm just a quiet, reasonably intelligent, average guy. How could I have screwed my life up this badly? There were periods in my twenties when I couldn't afford a cell phone. It's not that I ever couldn't afford to eat, though I certainly wasn't eating like a king by any means. I ate one piece of chicken a day with some rice. Every day. Occasionally I'd make Hamburger Helper and on those nights I actually did think that I was living like royalty. It was, for whatever reason, a big treat for me. Such a treat that I always ate far too much and got far, far too drunk in the process.

That was my life. I didn't have a phone. I was always just a few days away from having my electricity shut off. My internet was disconnected for non-payment. It was all just spiraling out of control. No matter how bad it got, though, I always had $30 every day for booze. I always had money for alcohol. The only thing that mattered to me.

It was like that for years. Alcohol was the only important thing. Everything else, including my life itself, was secondary at best. I started cutting again. Then I started swallowing pills. I used to swallow whole bottles of Tylenol or Advil while guzzling my second bottle of wine. Alone in the dark, in a stupor, I would write my suicide notes. Yes, that's plural. I wrote many, many suicide notes. I still have one in a filing cabinet in my home office right now. It's typed out and clean. I signed it by hand, of course. I actually wrote out the same damn suicide note so many times in my life that I finally decided I need a typed version written when I'm sober so that it's ready to go for when I finally go far enough to end it all.

The thing about my suicide notes is that they aren't "goodbye." No, my suicide notes have always been "I'm so sorry" with an explanation that 'something happened' in my life that I was never able to get past. I was never able to get over it. I tell them I've always been in pain. Intense, overwhelming, never-ending pain. I say that I'm sorry. I'm sorry that I failed in life. And then I lie and I describe a fake happy memory of my life. Something so that they'll think it wasn't all bad. That at least I went out with that one happy memory and that maybe that's where I'll go in the afterlife.

In my darkest moments I never believed that God would forgive me. I'd be drunk, cutting myself, sobbing, wailing into the void as I write my notes. Because deep down I feared that my whole family was going to heaven while I was going to hell I always needed an excuse to explain it all away. I wrote time after time after time that I wouldn't really be gone. It wasn't truly goodbye. That my spirit would always be walking the streets by the house where I grew up – that I'd always be there.

Even as I sliced a hunting knife into my flesh and swallowed a bottle of painkillers in what very well might have been my final moments in this life, I kept my secret. I couldn't let them know, even in death, what had happened or who I was.

I got so drained of writing that note over and over and over that I finally decided I may as well write it sober and make it coherent. Which is to say that, for years, I've had a suicide note available at the ready to fill that need for whenever I completed the act.

One night I had done these things to myself. I drank a bottle of vodka, which was certainly not my regular drink-of-choice, interspersed with a pack of beer. I drank myself beyond alcohol poisoning. I was completely annihilated drunk. I collapsed onto the floor and I lost consciousness. That should have been it. My life should have ended that night. I drank so much that my body was shutting down. I'll always remember the moment that something woke me up. Call it a guardian angel. Something pulled me back into this life at the last second. I felt my throat come back to life and managed to lift my head and roll over just in time to expel copious amounts of vomit. I power-puked for several minutes before falling over once more and losing consciousness again.

The next morning when I awoke to the most disgusting sight of my life, I was amazed at how clear my memory had been of that moment. It truly felt as though there had been some manner of intervention mere seconds before I choked and died on my own vomit. I should have died that night or one of a hundred other similarly appalling experiences, but I'm still here.

It took me a while to realize but one day it just popped into my head that I was alone. All of my friends were gone. They'd either moved away, gotten married and started families, or they'd just stopped talking to me. One of my best friends had moved half a continent away but he still came home for two weeks every summer. I knew that he was home and I'd been waiting for his call. It was his last day on vacation. He hadn't called. He wouldn't be calling. I was alone.

I started thinking about friends and friendships now in the distant past. It was only then that I realized one by one all of my friends had left my life. I thought we just hadn't gotten together in awhile. I must have been scared to admit it. They were gone. I'm not much of a fan of social media so I'd deactivated my Facebook account years ago. I logged back in and scrolled through page after page to see what my friends had been up to. There were photos of weddings I hadn't been invited to, babies I didn't know had been born, new houses, new jobs, new lives. Someone I thought was an old friend not only hadn't invited me to his wedding but I learned that he'd actually 'unfriended' me. That stung.

I don't blame him. I know why he did it. He lost a dear friend in a drunk driving incident years ago. I had begun driving drunk. I'd hop in the car after drinking all night and drive home. I'd drive to McDonald's for a burger. Sometimes I'd drive drunk to the liquor store to restock my supplies only minutes before closing time, just because I couldn't bear the thought of not having alcohol in my fridge. I was drunk driving on a regular basis. So it cost me at least one friendship. Probably more.

Realizing that my old friend wasn't going to call made me sit down and review some of the other friendships and relationships I'd lost over the years. There were many people who simply got up and walked out of my life. Sometimes they offered an explanation or an excuse. Other times they just moved further and further down on my list of recent texts and phone calls, until it sunk in for me that I'd been phased out. I can certainly understand why I lost those friendships. I was always anxious, depressed, nervous and decidedly negative. I have an unmatched ability to be negative. About everything. Which explains why people would eliminate me, consciously or unconsciously, from their social circle or peripheral attachments. I get it. Still, I can't quite move on from it.

I found myself thinking about a relationship which had unceremoniously ended. In the closing months of 2013 I'd started a relationship with a girl I'd met at that minimum wage job. She was the manager, actually. We were the same age and had gone to high school together. She'd always had a crush on me and this was her chance to have me. She knew that I was in the darkest chapter of my life and I think partly she wanted to take me on as a project and set me straight. Interestingly she had always felt like I was far beyond her league. That I was Mr. Popular and Mr. Cool Guy. Of course, I never had been, she just had that impression for reasons I don't fully understand.

There was one problem, though. She was married. Somehow I've managed to largely push this out of my mind and to completely let myself off the hook for these transgressions but it's time I finally admitted to some of my worst moral failings. In 2013 I had sex with a married woman. Two married women, actually. One of them was just some random woman I'd met on the internet. We had sex in a park on a picnic table. Her husband sat in their car and watched. I include that detail only because it speaks to how low my morality had plummeted. It's not that I'm proud of that fact, it's simply another example of my desperate need to have my ego stroked.

You can see, then, that having a pretty girl from my high school past re-emerge to continuously pump my tires with compliments was a temptation I couldn't forgo. I liked that she was married. It made me feel so much better about my own worth as a person that another man's wife was sneaking off with me.

I never thought that I would be someone who would participate in an extra-marital affair. After all, I was raised with strict christian ideals and beliefs. I'm not proud of what I did by any measure. I treated both Robyn and her husband so cruelly and selfishly that words cannot describe the magnitude of how morally bankrupt I had become. It made me feel better about myself to have sex with a married woman. That's the truth. I'm not defending it or trying to explain it away. I'm disgusted by it. I took advantage of her feelings for me and her desire to help me.

I was so evidently adrift at this point in my life. Robyn only wanted to help set me back on course toward happiness and the life I should have been leading. Sure, she wanted the sex and the excitement too, though I firmly believe those motivations were secondary to her desire to help an old friend who wasn't doing so well in life. She wanted to help me, while I happily began sleeping with her purely to inflate my own ego.

Robyn didn't do a great job of hiding our affair. I think she wanted to get caught. She told her husband she was spending time with me and that she'd been to my house. I haven't met any married couples where one partner could casually begin spending time at the home of a person of the opposite sex without this becoming something of an issue. I have no idea why Robyn told him, unless she wanted to raise a sense of alarm in him.

He was suspicious but he didn't do much. He looked the other way for months as she repeatedly came to my house for sex. Sometimes she even would have returned home to him with alcohol on her breath and undeniable evidence of sex on her body. Then one night there was a storm coming in and Robyn couldn't make it out of town to their country home. She lied to her husband and said she was going to spend the night with a female friend of hers. She was sitting next to me while talking to him on the phone. I remember hearing him say "Please. Just don't stay at *his* house."

The tone of his voice struck me. They'd been talking about me. How much did he know? Obviously he knew enough to be worried that Robyn was lying to him and that she'd actually be spending the night with me. When she got off the phone I insulted him. I ranted about him. I called him a 'beta male' who couldn't hold onto his wife. She laughed and said that he's well-below average endowment and 'bad in bed.' It all made me feel a sense of superiority.

So I fucked her right then and there, feeling powerful and confident, with her degradations and mockery of her husband still fresh in our minds. I'd been the one hurting for so long in life that I'd found a sense of protection in being the secret side-action guy. Not that it was ever much of a secret with Robyn openly talking about me. I just felt invincible in the situation. I wasn't the one who could be humiliated. I wasn't the one who could be perceived as sexually inadequate or weak. I was the guy fucking the married girl and hearing her cum for me. In some strange way, that meant I was protected. Shielded. I was safe from being hurt.

Of course I know now how very wrong all of that was. I absolutely was the weak person who should have known better than to spread such pain and emotional trauma to others. I should have known. Or perhaps I did and I simply chose to silence my better judgment.

After it had been going on for quite awhile, one afternoon Robyn came to me with fear in her eyes. She was visibly agitated and didn't know what to do. She was pregnant. I couldn't believe how low I'd sunk in life. I'd been sleeping with a married woman and now something that should have been such an exciting and happy time in their marriage was ruined. I even had the audacity to ask her what the chances were that her husband would just quietly carry on even if the child was mine. She said they hadn't been sleeping together for weeks. She vehemently argued the point that it had been so long since she'd allowed him to have sex with her that he would never believe that the child was his.

We discussed our options but both of us knew there was only one available course of action.

I had to scrounge up every dollar I could get my hands on to pay for her abortion. In doing so I felt like such a failure. I didn't think anything could bring me lower than what I had done to her. Robyn is a sweet, innocent person. Her only crime was falling for me and wanting to lift me up. What I did to her was truly terrible. I hated myself for it. I despised myself. I had an identity crisis as I truly wondered what sort of person I am. I thought I was a good person. I wanted to be a good person. But are these really the dilemmas which befall moral, honest, decent people?

I wallowed in heartache then swallowed as much booze as I could get my hands on. I didn't have the capacity for this kind of an event in my life. I already felt like I carried too much pain, baggage, and trauma. I selfishly wanted to put this behind me as quickly as I could and forget that it had ever happened. I wasn't willing to even hold myself accountable for this horrible moral failing.

Weeks later I got a message from Robyn's husband over social media. I'll never forget that message.

 "You fucked my wife!" he wrote. I do have to give him kudos for being concise and direct to the point.

I was devastated that he'd found out. It meant that I had to acknowledge my own wrongdoing. I wasn't just going to walk away unscathed and be able to pretend nothing had happened. I had to face the reality that I'm the person who slept with a married woman. I ended this marriage. I ruined their happiness. I hurt this guy in a way that will harm him for years. Maybe even forever. I'm *that* idiot. I'm that *jackass.* I'm the one who did this terrible, horrible thing. Here he is confronting me about it. So what am I going to do? Cry? Apologize? Tell him how sorry I am? Tell him he can punch me in the face until he feels better?

No. Because despite everything that I had done and despite my indisputable status as the offender here, I somehow still was able to hide behind the false ego which I so often presented as a mask before my true self. That false character which I outwardly presented as being the real me – that guy? – he's a fucking self-righteous, arrogant, jerk.

How would I handle this obviously aggrieved man coming to me to vent his frustrations and process his understandable anger toward me?

Well, I doubled down and I made everything even worse.

"You're welcome," I wrote back.

Robyn later told me that when he read my response her husband picked up his laptop and threw it into a wall with such force that the laptop had shattered. The wall needed to be fixed. Yet nothing was as broken as his heart and for the rest of my days I will always remember that I am the one who inflicted that pain. I'm not cocky and proud of myself anymore. Far from it. The last thing that I ever wanted was to be held accountable for what I knew to be immoral and indecent actions with Robyn. I couldn't handle the consequences of my own actions. I knew that when I was doing it. But I did it all anyway.

Inevitably, Robyn asked her husband to move out of their home. She wanted me to move in after he was gone but I refused. As if I hadn't been terrible enough, I realized that I didn't really care for Robyn all that much. I didn't want to be with her and to build a relationship with her. I just wanted to keep having sex with her for my own selfish reasons. Somehow I got away with that for two years. I continued sleeping with Robyn, once or twice having sex with another girl behind her back, all the while making it clear that there was no room for a long-term serious relationship.

In the end Robyn went out one year for Halloween dressed in lingerie. She didn't invite me to go with her. When she got to a bar she had her friend take pictures of her and they both texted photos to me. I realized my relationship with Robyn was over and that she was determined to hurt me as she walked out of my life. As the night went on I kept getting more and more texts and photos from both Robyn and her friend. She was dancing with other guys. She was letting them touch her ass and her boobs. They were forcing me to witness it, even if I wasn't there.

I got what I deserved in the end. She left me.

Of course I knew that any girl who will cheat *with* you will cheat *on* you. So I have no right to be upset or bothered by any of that conduct. We weren't even truly in a relationship, as I had so cruelly often said to her. I deserved every bit of that cruelty she inflicted on me in the end. Unquestionably. I deserved that.

I haven't heard from her since. It's been several years now and once she left I don't think she ever looked back. I have to admit that I look back, though. Frequently. I look back in bewilderment as I ponder: How did I treat Robyn so badly? Will I ever be in a place in my own life where I will be able to apologize? I hope so. I truly hope to someday be able to apologize.

Not all of my friendships ended so spectacularly. The theme is always the same though. Friends stop wanting to be around me and then they simply dart toward their exit. I've

seen it so many times it rarely catches me by surprise
anymore.

I was totally lost. I'd sunk so low from the good, respectable,
kind person I wanted to be.

Chapter 6
Therapy

I'd started seeing a therapist in 2013 when my life was in
shambles. After ending up in the psychiatric ward of the
hospital my visits to a therapist intensified. I'd been able to
admit to my therapist that I'd been scarred by childhood
sexual experiences, and even shared that they were
homosexual experiences. I'm able to casually type those
words out now under the implied safety of a pseudonym. The
reality, though, is that I barely got those words out when the
time came. I choked on each syllable. My eyes rotated from

the distant wall to the floor. I cried when I told the therapist about my past. There is simply too much pain and heartache, mixed with unprocessed thoughts and emotions, for me to be able to speak the words aloud with a clear voice. Somewhat adding to the tension, for me, was that I suspected my therapist to be gay so I spoke as diplomatically about that trauma as I could.

My therapist then made a point of telling me that his wife's name is "Susan" so I partially lowered my guard when it came to some aspects of that trauma. I knew he didn't have a wife. I knew the man was gay. I could feel it in my soul. It didn't matter in the slightest to me, aside from the added uncomfortableness of explaining to an obviously gay man that a homosexual past encounter had utterly gutted and destroyed me.

The therapist felt that I couldn't talk about those experiences until I stopped drinking. While I wanted to focus on 'fixing' the traumatic experiences and their effects all my therapist felt comfortable with was getting me sober. I don't fault him for that. I was obviously drinking far too much and my only coping mechanism was to get black-out drunk.

The therapist and I spent years in a stand-off. He tried to get me sober, I kept insisting the alcohol was a *de facto* psychological inertia. It was keeping me going, at least.

I was wrong — completely and absurdly wrong — but he just kept pushing me and pushing me toward getting sober. It took one therapy session per month from 2013-2015, then one session every two weeks for a time, before I finally went to an Alcoholics Anonymous meeting in 2015. I hated it. I didn't identify with the other people at AA. They had all experienced alcoholism so differently than I had. They had consumed alcohol during the day. They'd gone through failed marriages and divorce. Some of them had been to prison. One guy had even murdered a prostitute. I didn't connect with these people. I didn't feel like their struggle with alcohol compared to mine.

To appease my therapist I continued going to AA. I never spoke. I didn't make any friends there. I went in, listened, and I left.

After time my therapist called in reinforcements in the form of an addictions counselor. I suppose it was that counselor who removed any lingering doubts I may have had as to whether or not my drinking constituted a problem or an addiction. In discussing my drinking habits with her I recalled the number of times I made a mad dash to the store minutes before closing time to restock my wine or beer supplies, simply to ensure I had some alcohol available. I told her about how, when I'd fall into a stupor of intoxication, my main thought process would always be 'one more drink.' It didn't matter how much I had in me, I always kept drinking, insisting that I needed 'one more.'

In response, she told me that I was describing an "addict-style of thinking." I didn't like being categorized or grouped in with "addicts." I still don't. It's unfair of me in many ways, most of which are perhaps rooted in egotism. Yet I find a harsh connotation and stigma accompanies the term 'addict' which is bothersome in my view. It was therefore a difficult pill to swallow, pardon the phraseology, hearing an addictions counselor describe me in such terms. After all, I'm university educated. I can carry on a conversation with lawyers, accountants, artists, politicians, professors, or journalists. It was demeaning to find myself labeled with such a hurtful descriptor.

So much of addiction treatment includes these hurtful terms, phrases, and encouraged ways of viewing our own struggles. That same counselor gave me a small coin to carry with me, much like an AA chip, which had an inscription supposedly for my benefit. On one side it read "We can't change the direction of the wind but we can adjust our sails." That's a valuable motto which I find helpful and genuinely uplifting. However, the opposite side of the coin reads in thick block letters "ALTHOUGH I AM POWERLESS I AM NOT HELPLESS."

Why would I ever want to view myself as *powerless?* I simply don't view myself as being powerless. I consider myself to be, actually, quite powerful. I have the ability to learn, to improve, to communicate, to educate, to have compassion and empathy. I can stand up for myself. I can lead the way. I can do many things which are deserving of feeling gratified, accomplished, or capable. It's simply an erosion of my own self worth to describe myself as being *powerless* but such is the message and methodology of alcoholics anonymous and many of the treatment regimes which orbit their core teachings.

Alcoholics Anonymous is a religion. It is a religion exactly like every other religion any of us has ever encountered. There is the deity, the holy texts, and the religious doctrines which must be followed in order to be accepted within the religion. Alcoholics Anonymous presents itself as being 'the one true path to sobriety' but in actuality it is one of many paths to sobriety. It also has a much lower success rate than other paths, which I'll discuss later on.

At this point in my life I was confronted with a harsh but undeniable truth. I had a serious problem with alcohol. If I didn't change, my life story would be completely consumed by drinking. I can't stand that thought. I cannot accept being defined as *an alcoholic*. I do not and I will never accept that as a permanent label of shame to be etched upon my entire existence.

Yet, this is one of the principal requirements of the AA religion. 'Once an alcoholic, always an alcoholic.' This is what AA, of all places, teaches about alcohol abuse disorders. No. I refuse to accept the label of being an alcoholic. I refuse to allow that humiliation and indignity to overwrite every other aspect of my existence and my life. I am a person of many failings, failures, and absolute fuck-ups for which I owe more apologies than perhaps I can ever utter in the limited time that I have left in this life. "Alcoholic" does not define me. It will *never* define me. And it sure as sunrise will not become a self-degrading anchor which deprives me of my individuality, ability for personal growth, my own sense of identity, and whatever dignity I may feel that I continue to hold. I've done wrong. I've certainly abused alcohol and at times been chemically dependent upon it.

This does not make me a *permanent alcoholic* who must live in everlasting shame. Absolutely not.

Chapter 7
Drinker, Failure, Chip-on-the-Shoulder, Spy

A few years ago, while I was still drinking every single night, I applied to work as an intelligence officer for a national security-intelligence agency. Some people might do a double take or feel somewhat dumbfounded by that statement. After all, how did I ever expect to get the job? My credit rating was ruined. I couldn't successfully go longer than a day without alcohol. And at this point anyone who trifled through my internet history find some pretty compelling evidence to suggest that I have a thing for sexually dominant women.

All Russia would have to do is send a dominatrix to my house with some wine and money and I'd hand over nuclear secrets, right?

Well, no, I didn't really see it that way. For one thing I'm far too patriotic to ever betray my country. I'd die a poor, forgotten patriot before I'd ever choose to live as a wealthy traitor to my country. Being an intelligence officer is actually my dream job. If I could ever be relieved of my social anxiety it's a position for which I would bring a passion and a broad skill set. Plus, I'd never be bored again. With these motivations in mind, I set my drinking problem aside and focussed on all of the reasons why this was the right career path for me.

The agency in question gave me very clear instructions not to reveal anything about their hiring policies and procedures. Seeing as how it would take them about an hour to defeat the privacy shield of the pseudonym I have utilized for this story, it would be most unwise for me to ignore their requests. So I won't name the agency itself and I won't get into any details that aren't already common knowledge or publicly available facts.

I made it quite far in the hiring process. I got through the background checks, the written exams, days-long interviews with high ranking intelligence officers, and other assessment techniques which took a great deal of impromptu decision-making. It was quite serious and intense. It was also a lot of fun. I made it all the way through the process up to the point where I had to meet with a psychologist who worked for this agency. The next step was a polygraph to determine if I'd lied to them at any step of the game.

Somehow I knew that I was never going to sneak my alcohol abuse by a psychologist. If alcohol even came up in the conversation my goose was cooked. It wasn't until I was being interviewed by that psychiatrist that I came face to face with my own fraudulence.

She asked me "Are you a good liar, sir?" I felt embarrassed. I hung my head downward, readjusted in my chair and said "No. No I'm not."

Ironically though, I knew I was putting on an act. I was pretending to be someone else with fake emotions and a fake answer. At that moment I wasn't even sure of the truthful answer.

Am I a good liar?

Actually, I think I am, but only in small doses. I don't think I could spin a web of lies that would keep others off a true scent for any length of time. I am capable, however, of pulling off some deceptions for short intervals of time. I can be a completely different person for a 5 hour flight. Put me in the seat next to someone for 5 hours and I can convincingly become someone else. But put me next to that same person a week later for a 3-day conference and I'm tapped out. I've already expended my deceptive currency. I can't keep a big lie going for a long time. I mean, I also don't know if *anyone* can. I simply know that I can't. Creating a mask or a characterized version of yourself is exhausting. Absolutely exhausting.

I know this because every waking moment outside of my home is an energy-draining act of theater. I have never shown my true self. To anyone. I have kept that true self hidden in the depths of my past. There is too much vulnerability. Too much pain and weakness. On top of it all, I spent years softly questioning 'Am I a psychopath?'

To be asked by a highly trained psychologist employed by a security-intelligence partner of the Five Eyes is a tad daunting.

The honest answer to her question should have been "I don't know – I don't even have a frame of reference from which to begin answering you truthfully." Because I didn't, at the time.

That psychiatrist saw right through me. I'm an impeccable judge of what other people are thinking based upon barely perceptible facial movements and even the slightest body gestures. The eyes and lips are far more communicative than a person's words. I saw it on her face that I hadn't fooled her one bit. She probably could have told me right then and there what's psychologically wrong with me and that I needed treatment for alcohol addiction. She knew. Even though I don't fully know myself, I could tell that she had figured me out.

Ultimately, she saved me from ascending to a position which I would have done poorly despite my every effort. If I'd gotten the job there's no doubt in my mind that it would have ended badly for me. Imagine becoming an intelligence officer tasked with safeguarding your country against malignant foreign actors while masking a secret alcohol dependence, having little or no sense of self, and being internally governed by an overwhelming desire to prove your value to an omnipotent deity who still loathes you for your childhood. I'm not sure that these are the foundational elements of a successful real-life James Bond. Especially if this particular James Bond is only capable of seducing women who are already married.

Chapter 8
Alcoholics Anonymous

I'm already ashamed. I am, truly. I'm not proud of virtually anything I've done while I was drinking. It's a dark, loathsome chapter of my past which I seek to overcome. I kept trying to avoid becoming a member of Alcoholics Anonymous but the reality is that it continued to be held out as my only real option to improve. Alcoholics Anonymous embraces the same shame, negativity, and self-loathing as the preacher in that gospel hall basement. This is partly why AA didn't sit well with me. I believe that one can become healed of both of the underlying issues which led them toward alcohol abuse as well as healed from alcohol abuse disorders.

I do not accept that someone who abused alcohol for one year of their life and has not had a single alcoholic beverage in twenty years is *still* an alcoholic. I do not accept that such a person needs to be named, shamed, degraded, and labeled with a slur. 'Alcoholic' *is* a slur.

I fully understand and recognize that I abused alcohol. I fully understand and recognize that I am a person with alcohol abuse disorder, at this time. Yet it is my genuine and emphatically held belief, based upon actual science rather than religion, that persons such as myself can become healed of alcohol abuse disorder. I will not *always and forever* be a person afflicted with these poor coping mechanisms. I will improve and adapt. I will grow spiritually. I will expand my emotional depths, horizons, and dimensions. I can – and I will.

I have lived a life of darkness far too long. I reject the notion that this is an inevitable progression toward my destruction. No. I will live a life in the light – and I will find joy, happiness, and peace. I will do these things without being branded irrevocably as an alcoholic.

Alcoholics Anonymous is little more than a failed religious sect whose principal recruiting technique is to etch in irreversible ink a shame, humiliation, and libelous label which brow-beats believers into long-term commitment. If you tell a person continuously and convincingly that they are *always and forever* an alcoholic, who ought to feel great shame, but that your community church group is the sole place which may grant them reprieve and dignity perhaps they will come back meeting after meeting after meeting. For that minor dignity you allow from a deity you define in malleable, circumstantial, terms.

Or maybe science, with its vastly more effective treatment regime, is the better option for literally everyone under the age of 70.

It isn't my intention to criticize Alcoholics Anonymous or anyone who has ever walked the path of the 12 steps. I've met very happy and genuinely kind people through AA who attribute their sobriety to that program. I'm happy for them and for all of the people across the world who have found fellowship, acceptance, healing, and sobriety through Alcoholics Anonymous.

For anyone reading these words, if you struggle with alcohol abuse or if your drinking is out of control, I do sincerely and strongly recommend attending an AA meeting and hearing their message. Some people have found sobriety, happiness, and contedness from AA. I would never want to deprive anyone of that. If you struggle with alcohol addiction, abuse, or dependency: Go to your nearest AA meeting as quickly as you can. There you will find a lay-person group of people who have found sobriety and who hold a vast collective wealth of knowledge on matters of spiritual, psychological, and medical relevance.

If you are hurting from alcohol and you can't stop drinking: Go to AA, your doctor, your pharmacist, your spouse, and every person in your life whom you trust to care for you and your well-being.

AA didn't work for me though I would like to explain to you why I came to that conclusion. It wasn't until I was actually sober that I realized AA doesn't work for me. The only requirement for membership in AA is 'a desire to quit drinking.' I had a desire to quit drinking, so I was able to go into AA meetings and to formally join an AA group in my area. I was never sober though. I've attended AA meetings drunk, buzzed, or with a case of beer waiting for me in the trunk of my car. I didn't exactly advertise any of those facts to anyone but I feel like it's a relevant detail in my story. I've been attending Alcoholics Anonymous meetings for years and it did very little to help me to achieve sobriety.

As a newcomer to AA the first thing you'll notice is that the organization feels like Freemasonry-lite, with a great deal more Christian theology. There are Masonic symbols scattered about and certain rituals that give the organization a decidedly Masonic decorum. Which is fine, I'm certainly not complaining about that. My knowledge of the Freemasons is limited to recognizing a few of their basic symbols, which are pridefully placed throughout AA meeting places. *(I hold no opinions, positive or negative, toward Freemasons – and I take them at their word that they are decent people with community-minded aspirations).*

Over time you'll start to realize that AA is established very much like a religion. There is a God whom they call your "higher power." There is a Bible which they call "The Big

Book." There are other sacred texts such as "the Daily Reflections" etc. There is a high priest, Bill Wilson the founder of AA, and disciples Dr. Bob etc. The 12 steps are highly religious rituals. The secret healing power of AA is the healing cleanse offered by your higher power through acknowledgement of past wrongs, repentance, and commitment to "keep coming back" as is often said at the conclusion of each meeting, right after a group recitation of the Lord's Prayer.

AA is a religion for people with alcohol abuse disorders and which has expressly avoided the label of religion to avoid offending those who blame God for their problems with alcohol. Which is fair, because a great many people in AA foster resentment toward the religions they were raised in or the God they feel neglected or abandoned them in their alcoholism.

At the end of the day, AA's solution to alcohol abuse is just God, prayer, and to continue seeking God and praying. That's it. That's the "simple program" as they call it.

AA is nearing 100 years old. As an organization they are heavily resistant to change. Their sacred texts are, much like the versions of the Bible you'd find in Christian churches, written in a temporally specific cadence. Much has changed since the 1930s. Our modern language is much different. Women occupy a markedly different place within our society. Our peoples and cultures are different.

Our scientific knowledge and abilities are different.

Despite all of this, AA remains unchanged nearly a century after its founding. This is not a new argument that I am making. In 2015 *the Atlantic* published a piece entitled *The Irrationality of Alcoholics Anonymous* which capably and powerfully describes the flaws of AA's core mentality and teachings.

Throughout human history we have always looked for religious-type answers to complex mysteries or unexplainable events. It's difficult to understand why someone like me who knows that alcohol is so dangerous and destructive for themselves would continue to drink. What could be making all of these people ruin their lives and the lives of their loved ones with alcohol?

AA's answer is simple: Alcohol is "cunning, baffling, and powerful."

Not exactly the scientific explanation you were hoping for? Well, AA doesn't offer scientific solutions. AA is an ancient religious prescription to a problem that had yet to be solved by science. AA might as well tell those suffering from alcohol addiction to look out into the sea and ask Poseidon to free them from alcoholism. It would make as much scientific sense as referencing alcohol as if it were an evil consciousness actively strategizing away while lurking behind us, just waiting to make us drink that next glass of wine.

Religion isn't the answer to curing alcohol abuse disorders. People are dying, going to prison, or losing their entire lives to this fatal affliction. What other disease which destroys the lives of millions of people around the world each year would we solve by telling everyone to pray harder?

I don't begrudge AA or criticize anyone who has found benefit from its message or its fellowship. I can only say this: I attended AA meetings for over 5 years and it never helped me to get sober. For me, it just didn't work. What I often found in AA were groups of people who have been sober for 10 years. 15 years. Sometimes even 20 years or more. I didn't find value in listening to people who've been sober for 20 years. I don't feel like they really understand me and my struggle with alcohol, and I don't understand them.

AA preaches that once an alcoholic, always an alcoholic. You must wear that label for life. That label — alcoholic — which is a slur and an insult to so many is mandatory in AA. Mandatory and permanent. It is a badge of dishonor and shame which AA thrusts upon its members.

I don't welcome or support that. For one, I don't believe that 'alcoholic' is a fair term to apply across the board. It means something different to each person using the term. We aren't all the same, either. There are many different types and degrees of alcohol use disorders. One blanket term isn't quite fair, particularly where the term carries such a negative stigma. It's a humiliation and one which AA wants you to own forever.

AA is highly dogmatic on this and other elements of its doctrine. I've even heard AA service workers criticize speakers for saying "Hi, I'm Bob and I'm an alcoholic." The AA service workers say the 'alcoholic' confession is more important than your name so you should always begin with "Hi. I'm an alcoholic and my name is Bob." Imagine. Their number one priority is the shame of alcohol use disorder. Who you are as a person is secondary to your group shaming.

The numbers speak for themselves. AA has an abysmally-low success rate in helping people to stay sober. To try the same program again and again is a cruelty in itself. I felt there had to be a better way. In the 21st century 'just go to church and pray' can't possibly be the best medical or scientific advice to people whose lives are on the line.

I found that better way forward — my unbreakable faith and belief in God tells me that it was no accident that I found this better way forward — and I'm sharing my story with you so that anyone still suffering from alcohol abuse can get the proper help that they need.

Chapter 9
Justice

My alcohol abuse continued unabated until just a few years
ago. People often say that those suffering from addiction
need to hit 'rock bottom' before they will change. This was
my rock bottom moment in my history of alcohol abuse. This
is a very difficult story for me to tell. I am so ashamed of
what happened that I wrote about the event with a sarcastic
tone lingering in my mind. Please know that I don't treat
these events lightly. These themes of childhood trauma,
addiction, mental health, and related social infractions –
these topics are near and dear to my heart. I take each of
them exceptionally seriously. I do, at times, struggle to work
my way through some of these topics and sometimes resort
to utilizing a sarcastic tone.

My inability to communicate entirely professionally
regarding certain traumatic events should not be interpreted
as a lack of sincerity or remorse. I assure you that I know
when and where I have done wrong, and I am sorry for all of
it. I am tortured by each and every little memory of anything
and everything that I have done wrong. I know my faults and

have enumerated them precisely, though privately in many respects.

There is no worse betrayal than a betrayal between brothers. I'm not trying to be poetic. I'm simply trying to explain. I have a few brothers. I had another brother who I lost. He wasn't biologically my brother, no. For me, though, he'd been around since the day I opened my eyes. He was always there, always a part of the family. He's always been family.

I'd had my suspicions for about a year. For a year I silently observed and took mental notes. There were little indications here and there that my 'brother' wasn't who he was pretending to be. Though I was the only one who had noticed. I'm the invisible ghost-child, remember? Nobody was going to listen to me about anything of relevance. They all preferred to pretend that I was entirely inept. Which is how everyone in my family treats me. I'm just some dumb, useless person, to be looked down upon and belittled if acknowledged at all.

Imagine my discomfort then, as a shy and socially anxious introvert, to have noted the many minor inconsistencies and contradictions in my brother-in-law's casual commentary. It was me – the person my family is least likely to listen to –

who obtained concrete evidence that my sister's husband had done something heinous and unforgivable. The details of that transgression are a separate story entirely.

Learning of his misdeeds and how he'd deeply hurt people I care about sent me into a terrible rage. There is something about being betrayed by someone so close to you which exacerbates exponentially any emotional wound. I am beyond embarrassed to admit that this betrayal by my brother-in-law led to my absolute lowest moments in alcohol abuse. My psychological composure was, to put it mildly, compromised.

I wasn't able to contain myself at all. After learning of my brother-in-law's misdeeds I began drinking uncontrollably. I had been drinking so heavily that I was actually consuming about 3 bottles of wine every night after work *before* 6:30pm. I was going to bed by 8:00pm and getting up at 5:00am to go work it all out at the gym. I had to drink two Powerades every morning at the gym and sometimes a third before going to the office. I don't know how I lived through this, truthfully, as I frequently popped extra-strength Tylenol PM in the evenings.

This is how I lived throughout January, February, and March of that year. For three months I was drinking three bottles of wine every single night. My skin turned pale. I had deep bags and wrinkles under my eyes. My eyes were constantly bloodshot. I was a wreck. On top of the damaging effects from that much drinking over such a long period of time I also inflicted a heavy toll on my own mental health by allowing myself to be totally and completely enraged every single night. I'd drink, listen to aggressive music, and angrily charge around my house in a huff, occasionally envisioning physically attacking my brother-in-law while throwing a fist into a wall. I punched things, I broke things, I swung a golf club around in the air as if it meant something. More than one light fixture lay shattered on the floor the next morning when I awoke in an enduring self-loathing.

I was falling apart and I knew it. My psychological and emotional state was truly alarming. Despite all of this I continued to show up for work day after day. If anyone had noticed anything they certainly never said a word to me. The only person who had commented on my change in behavior was a woman in my office who belonged to the same gym where I was now sweating out bottles of toxins each morning. She told some of our colleagues that I'd started going to the gym each morning because I was 'obsessed' with her. She's hot and looks great in yoga pants, but I hadn't even noticed she was there. My whole world was beginning to unravel. I wasn't going to the gym to see my hot coworker in her sports bra and yoga pants. I was going to the gym because if I didn't spend an hour on the treadmill sweating it all out then I was not going to be able to physically function and make it to the office. I was there out of physical necessity as a direct result of my alcohol dependency.

That's where I was psychologically only a few years ago. Psychotic, deranged, and unhinged.

That spring I started to settle down. My sister filed for divorce and my rage began to subside. Nobody ever found out how dark those three months had been for me. I wasn't the primary focus for my family and I had been entirely isolated from everyone else. I spent those three months alone, often in the dark, with my wine and my rage.

The spring was looking more positive. I reduced my alcohol intake, improved my sleep, and regained control of my emotions. At least enough to function in daily life without drawing attention to myself. I'd even started to look a bit healthier. Color had started to come back into my skin and I didn't have bloodshot eyes every day anymore. I was still drinking far too much and I knew it, though progress had clearly been made.

***

My older brother was getting married. I was deeply honored to be asked to be his best man. Nobody in my family knew that I had developed a very serious alcohol problem. Certainly, none of them knew that at this point I was incapable of leaving my house without a high-quantity of alcohol within my system. None of them knew. Yet, I somehow just expected that at least my closest brother would intuitively, somehow, figure it out.

He didn't.

I remember asking my brother why they had chosen such a remote location to get married. There were no taxis, public transit, and no hotels in the area. It meant that people either couldn't drink or there were going to be plenty of people driving home after drinking. I had remarked "This is just a recipe for me to get a DUI."

It's astonishing that I would think in such terms. Being in a remote location didn't mean *don't drink.* To me it meant that *drinking would be more dangerous here.*

Sobriety was so foreign to me that it never even crossed my mind as being an actual option. For my own brother's wedding.

I made a plan for myself. I picked up Coors Light for the wedding reception. It was going to be a very low key event. The wedding would be immediately followed by a garden party reception at a neighboring property. My family was refusing to attend since they knew alcohol would be a part of the evening. So at least I had *them* off my back. I would have six Coors Light beers while I ate, socialized, and did my part. Then I would leave after enough of the beers had worn off that it wasn't going to be an issue.

Yes, my brilliant plan to avoid driving drunk was in fact to drink six beers and then drive. This is how warped my mind had become at this point.

Even with 'a plan' in place, my evening did not go well. Perhaps being locked in my house for three months drinking three bottles of wine per ... afternoon... had not been a good set-up for me at this wedding. Perhaps.

My plan didn't exactly work out. You know, my brilliant plan which involved drinking six beers and eating a light dinner? Yeah, that plan somehow didn't work out. Firstly, I forgot to do the *eating* part and then I went a little heavy on the *drinking*. Then the event ended an hour earlier than planned. So rather than have supper, 6 beers, and then drive about 5 hours after starting to drink; I hadn't eaten, I drank 9 beers, and it had been closer to 4 hours since I'd started drinking.

Just in case you weren't convinced enough already that my night was about to go sideways, all of this was happening on a regional 'drunk driving enforcement weekend.' Every cop within a five hour drive of my hometown was on duty setting up roadside checks for drunk drivers.

I don't say it this way to be glib or in any way disrespectful. It's just a simple reality. I was absolutely hammered that night and I knew it. I chose to drive anyway because the wedding reception was held in a very small rural community and I had no way of getting home. I had no other way of getting my car home, which is a lame and illegitimate excuse for such reckless behavior. When you drink too much for too long this sort of decision-making actually holds up as being logical. People often opine that society should dramatically increase the criminal consequences for crimes typically committed by addicts.

In my own humble opinion, that's utter nonsense. The penalty can be $1 or $1,000,000. To someone suffering from addiction you may as well be speaking in terms of comets in a distant galaxy. None of it will resonate. It's nowhere near as powerful as the addiction which has completely infected that person's ability to think and rationalize. I speak from experience. I drove home drunk from bars hundreds of times in full view of uniformed police officers simply because I reasoned that leaving my car behind ran the risk of a $25 parking ticket.

A $25 parking ticket equals one case of beer. Do you really think I'm going to take the risk of losing a case of beer? Not a chance. Yes, I'll risk my life. Yes, I'll risk the safety of others. Yes, I'll risk going to prison. But, no, I will not risk losing a case of beer.

That's exactly the logical mechanics which were at play at that wedding reception. Not only had I not eaten dinner at the wedding but I didn't eat so much as a piece of cheese or a cracker. I meant to but somehow the time snuck away from me and the drinks kept flowing. The event was formatted in such a way that you were never anchored to a specific table with a meal to be presented. It was more casual with guests moving around, drinking, and expected to find their way to a buffet table at some point. I placed such a priority on the drinking that I never did make it to a buffet table.

Suddenly, the event was over and it was time to leave. I realized that I was drunk. I realized that I hadn't eaten anything all day. I didn't want to admit to anyone how much alcohol I had consumed, or that I so foolishly prioritized drinking above eating, or that as a grown adult I had put myself in this predicament. I was far from home. As a person without any friends, I was of course attending the event alone. I had nowhere to stay, nowhere to go, and I ran the risk of being found-out for my raging addiction. So I hopped in my car and began driving back to my own city.

I planned to stop at Subway on my way home. I figured I would eat a sandwich, drink some water, take some time and I'd be sober for the drive home. The Subway restaurant was only about a ten minute drive through rural backgrounds which should have been all but empty.

Before going to the wedding I had promised myself that I would eat dinner that night. I downloaded an app with a blood alcohol content calculator. I even used it in advance to get a sense of what my maximum alcohol intake could be. I told myself that I would be responsible. I told myself that I would eat, drink in moderation, and drink responsibly. The app on my phone was meant to be an independent gauge to ensure I wasn't putting anyone at risk. It wasn't a superb plan. It wasn't an ironclad plan by any definition. Some might even say the plan itself was patently absurd. Still, that was the plan. A plan I truly wish I'd adhered to, even partially.

If only it was that simple for people with alcohol abuse disorders. People like me.

The sad truth is that around this point in my history, I couldn't control how much I drank. Once I started there was no stopping until I blacked out. My very last action every night, year after year, would be to go searching for one more drink. One more drink. It didn't matter how drunk I was. It didn't matter if I was within an inch of alcohol poisoning. It didn't matter if it was 3:00am and I was on my third bottle of wine for the evening and I had a very important meeting with my boss first thing in the morning. None of it mattered. I always needed *one more drink.*

So there I was on an empty stomach, having consumed more than double the number of drinks I'd told myself would be safe, driving on dark country roads not far from my hometown. Driving along blaring outdated music I rounded a corner, rolled down a hill, and unknowingly sailed toward a collision with destiny. Over the next hill I could see the most horrifying sight for anyone in my position: the sparkling glow of red and blue lights.

A police unit – a half dozen of them in fact.

Up ahead there were two local police cruisers along with four cruisers from the department of Highway Safety. It was a spot check, straight ahead, with nowhere else to turn. Behind me there was another police cruiser which approached and activated its emergency lighting systems. I was trapped. Totally and completely trapped.

I felt a sharp panic as I sat motionless in my car that night. I did all of the obvious things that a drunk driver would do in that situation. I rolled down all four windows. I turned the air vents on high to blow the smell of alcohol out of the car. I put on my seatbelt. I checked for breath mints in the dash. The officer behind me must have felt like a fox who had a chicken simply fly right into its mouth.

Ahead of me was a platoon of law enforcement waving cars through one at a time. Behind me were more law enforcement officers coming to join the show. To my left there was a deep ditch and a barbed wire fence marking the perimeter to a cattle grazing field. To my right, another field of cattle. No escape. None.

I was surrounded by people with guns, tasers, pepper spray, and a mandate to nab some drunks behind the wheel. I wasn't exactly making it difficult for them to get results. My heart sank as I moved closer to the squadron of law enforcement vehicles with their lights flashing and cops standing in the roadway holding flashlights and orange glowing sticks.

Nothing feels worse than knowing you're about to be caught in your own stupidity. It was more than getting caught in my own stupidity, though. I was going to be discovered and revealed for the horrible, immoral person I had become. I was an addict. An alcohol-dependent mess. An embarrassment. I was unworthy of being loved; unworthy of life itself. It was all crashing down on me at once in an overwhelming wave of emotion. Waiting for the grand discovery of that moment made my stomach churn. I had to just keep moving toward them one inch at a time. Slowly.

There was a line of cars waiting to get through. I knew it was going to take several minutes. A few more minutes of sitting with the windows down and the air vents blasting, hoping the smell of my crime would waft away and I'd somehow manage to skulk by undetected. These might be my last moments of freedom. The last time I ever possessed a license to drive a vehicle.

It was unquestionably my darkest moment. I was face to face with a day of reckoning. I would be caught momentarily. I would be arrested and charged. I would be thrown in jail and then brought before a judge. I would be humiliated. My name would be published in the papers and on the news sites. My life would be over. It was too much. Far, far too much. I couldn't handle that shame and humiliation.

I don't think I could even survive a night in jail. If there had been a gun in the car with me that night I would have eaten a bullet before I would have reached the police roadblock up ahead. Suicide started to seem like my only option. The only way out of that predicament.

As my mind rapidly turned toward those thoughts, I felt a powerful force reach out and encapsulate me. It was a presence I'd felt before. A familiar presence. An energy, a voice, a compilation of messages and emotion.

It was the holy spirit. God Almighty.

He was there with me in the car that night. There is no question that my adrenaline was pumping and that my brain was highly activated from the fear, the perceived threat, the desire to escape, and of course the copious amount of alcohol in my blood. I cannot scientifically demonstrate that what I experienced that night was actually an encounter with an all-knowing, omnipotent, omnipresent being. I can't prove it. Yet, in my heart I wholly and completely know that what I am saying is true. It was real.

God himself came to sit in that car with me and await the impending arrest.

As soon as I felt his presence I started begging him to please let me off the hook. Please, somehow have those police officers neglect to check my car. Convince them not to check me for signs of impairment. Through divine intervention, somehow impede their ability or desire to notice me. I begged for a miracle. Anything. I pleaded and pleaded. I wasn't asking for sobriety. I wasn't asking to be dealt with fairly in the judicial system. I was asking God to save me from the consequences of my crime against society. I was asking to be saved from justice so that my behaviors and my alcohol abusive lifestyle could continue. It was not by any measure a noble or enlightened request on my part.

I knew that I couldn't handle the actual consequences of my actions. Inside, my inner dialogue with myself remains stunted as a child. My emotional constitution has thus far remained inseparably linked to that young child who I was all those years before sitting across the hall from that old preacher. In many ways, I am still that child, frozen in time, unable to move, unable to mature and develop into the person I should have grown into. I was nothing more than a childlike, emotionally fragile, scared, alcohol abuser. I didn't have the capacity to handle the full consequences of my actions. I would have died.

Everything in my being turned onto a trajectory toward suicide that night. Death was my only remaining option.

I couldn't handle the public humiliation of being charged and convicted with drunk driving. I would lose my job if I had been convicted and established a criminal record. My family would disown me. Nobody would ever date me after Googling me and finding the results. Everything was about to fall apart. My mind raced through each of the painful, overwhelming consequences while I was begging God for any kind of an escape. Any possible alternative. Suddenly, I felt a calming reassurance. I felt God's answer to my prayers there in the moment.

He wasn't telling me that I was off the hook. He was telling me that this simply needed to happen, but that it would be alright. I would be okay in the end. I could never truly describe the energy and the connection that I felt to the universe around me. It was a moment which existed outside of time where I knew the story of my life was about to change forever. God spoke in a pure light which permeated my heart and my mind. He told me that I was going to be caught, arrested, and charged. He told me that it needed to happen. That *I* needed for this to happen.

My heart sank beneath my feet. It was the worst outcome I could have imagined. At the time, I was scared and I felt abandoned. God had the power to help me but he wasn't going to. I could feel it. Yet, strangely, I also knew that God was telling me that I needed this. It was an intervention of sorts. He was telling me that if I didn't get arrested that night that I would be worse off somehow. That escaping this situation would only lead to a worse outcome for me. Inching my way closer and closer to my own demise, I knew that God who sat with me in the car that night was going to allow me to be arrested. But that he would spare me a criminal conviction.

God knew what I could handle and what would push me over the edge. He gave me a wake up call, not a death sentence. I knew what was going to happen. I knew it with every fiber of my being. God himself had let me feel just an ounce of what lay ahead. He didn't show me the future, yet he allowed me to know that there still was a future and that I would be in a better place when I got there.

When it was finally my turn at the front of the line of cars a young police officer approached me. Destiny was upon me. My moment of humiliation and shame had arrived. The officer stuck his face right up into my open window and without saying a word he began to grin. Immediately he knew that he'd caught me red-handed. He could smell the alcohol coming off me from feet away before he even got to the car. The rest was a simple formality.

"Have you been drinking tonight?" he asked me. I would later come to learn his name as officer Connors. A nice enough, well-built guy.

There was no sense in denying the obvious and at least I knew well enough not to completely lie to the police. "I had a beer," I replied with a partial truth.

Not that any other answer would have helped me but I would later learn that my answer was, shall we say, totally idiotic. By admitting that I'd had "a beer" I had given the police a legal basis to ask me to provide a breath sample into a breathalyzer. Of course, there was no escaping it at that point, but it was nice of me to accidentally help them build their case.

I didn't know it at the time but as it turns out there are a limited number of mobile breathalyzers for my local police to use. Since they had every available car and cop out setting up roadblocks, this particular police spot-check didn't have any equipment available to test my blood alcohol content. They didn't have a breathalyzer on hand. The young officer quickly arrested me and whisked me off to a nearby police station. Before driving off the police read to me what most people would know as a Miranda warning/constitutional caution. Or, colloquially, they read my rights.

Although I was heavily intoxicated and awash in shame and self-loathing, some default programming kicked in as a last defense mechanism. I immediately responded to the Miranda warning that I wanted to talk to my lawyer. These innocent few verbal exchanges meant more than I could ever know. A simple drunken mumble that I wanted to speak to my lawyer may as well have been the difference between life or death.

When we arrived at the police station I asked for my cell phone to contact my lawyer. The police refused to allow me any access to my cell phone, claiming that it was now "evidence." How a phone could be used as evidence in a drunk driving arrest I will never know. It's just a phone. A phone within which many inappropriate photos and also the phone number for my lawyer are stored. Still, it's just a locked cell phone.

I wasn't asking for my phone because I wanted to play Candy Crush or whatever I was specifically asking to call my lawyer,

James Patterson. I wasn't about to take a breathalyzer test without first speaking to my lawyer. Who knows, maybe there's some little-known legal loophole that could have saved me? I was still clinging to that faint hope.

The police not only wouldn't give my phone back to me but they wouldn't even let me use a phone at all. They said that they would call my lawyer on my behalf. Sitting in a small interrogation room, still locked in handcuffs, there was nothing that I could do to protest their overly authoritarian control over the situation. All I could do was watch as the police used an *expired* phone book from a year or so prior to look up the phone number for my lawyer.

Most people, including myself, probably didn't even realize phone books had an expiration date at all. Or if they did have an expiry date it was just universally accepted as being 2005 when virtually all of society stopped using phone books entirely.

Nevertheless, this was how the police determined they would make my most important phone call — on my behalf — all the while ignoring my protestations and insistence that I have my lawyer's cell phone number programmed into my phone. The police didn't care. They simply called the number from the expired phone book to check it off their list and say that they had honored my right to contact my lawyer.

It was late in the evening and on the weekend. Of course my lawyer wasn't at his office, which would be the only number you'd find for him in an outdated phone book. The police knew that their bare minimalist effort to contact my lawyer would certainly fail. They simply didn't care if I got to speak to my lawyer or not. So far as they were concerned, I was obviously guilty and everything else was just performative theater.

Much debate was had between myself and the police regarding contacting my lawyer. Since the police refused to actually try to contact James Patterson, I demanded they call another lawyer friend of mine, Mark James. In my hometown, Mark James is a very well known and prestigious lawyer. He doesn't handle criminal cases, however. Still, he's a lawyer who I could trust and his legal instincts would certainly be better than mine. I'd take any lawyer who I knew and trusted at that point. It was really beginning to unsettle me that the police seemed motivated to impede me from speaking to a lawyer at all.

When I said Mark's name, police constable Connors arrogantly replied "I've never heard of him." He was trying to be dismissive which really was off the mark for anyone in my town. I snickered in response.

"Yeah? He's a senior partner at the most prestigious law firm in the city," I retorted. I may have been a chronic drunk for 12 years but I still had some powerful drinking companions and I didn't mind bragging about it to a rookie cop who seemed determined to isolate me from legal counsel.

I rolled my eyes at the cop who smugly believed he'd scored an easy arrest and would celebrate with a beer with his buddies later on. On the inside I may have been a deeply unsettled, emotionally-stunted child screaming in fear. Outwardly, the false persona I wore as a mask – that alternate version of myself was able to maintain my confidence. My intellectual abilities remained sharp even though my neck was dangerously close to the noose. Officer Connors stuck to his nonchalant dismissive attitude. Connors didn't care one bit if I got to speak to my lawyer or not.

After an hour or so of arguing back and forth Connors simply dialed up the court-appointed freebie lawyer on duty and handed me the phone. After all, in his mind, all he had to do was check off a box saying I'd spoken to *"a"* lawyer. He dubiously checked off the box to his own satisfaction.

Having been forced to speak to a legal aid lawyer, I had no other cards to play. There was nothing else to stand in the way of the inevitable. I had to take a breathalyzer. This is where my confidence broke. I seriously doubted I would pass. I held out some hope, knowing I'd stalled things for a significant period of time since I arrived at the police station. All I could do was silently pray that God would let me walk out of there. As I prepared to provide a breath sample for the machine two police officers berated me.

One officer shouted at me not to "chew" on the device as if I were some kind of rabid raccoon. They threatened me that if I didn't keep blowing air from my lungs hard enough or long enough that they would charge me with various other crimes. As I inhaled a deep breath and held the breathalyzer tube in my hands the police threatened to charge me with "refusal to provide a breath sample." They shouted this quite literally as I was in the process of providing the breath sample. As I continued exhaling into the device, the second officer in the room barked that they were going to add 'obstruction of justice' to their list of charges against me.

Obstruction of justice and refusal to provide a breath sample
– as I provided a breath sample.

I found out later that the police were worried I'd sobered up
while sitting in the interrogation room and they'd actually
shifted their own strategy to wanting to charge me with
refusing to cooperate, rather than continuing to pursue a
drunk driving charge. Shouting at me as I blew into the
device was apparently an intimidation tactic, hoping to scare
me so much that I couldn't complete the task. It didn't
matter to them that I was following all of their instructions.
They just wanted to nail me with something. It didn't seem
to matter what that conviction may be.

I had to sit and await the breathalyzer results for about ten
minutes. As it turned out the police were worried for
nothing. I had not sufficiently sobered up. I was almost
double the legal limit, according to their breathalyzer. I
broke down and sobbed as officer Connors told me I was
being charged with drunk driving and would spend the night
in jail. My whole world came crashing down that night. I'd
spent years hiding the fact that I had a drinking problem. I'd
been hiding so much of my mental health and my personal
challenges. I felt like I just lost one little thing after another

and now I was losing all that's left. My dignity, my self respect, my honor. Even my own sense of self. It was all being taken from me.

I didn't want Connors to take me to jail. I just wanted him to shoot me. I looked up at him slowly. My eyes fixated on his service pistol. He could just end this. He could end my miserable, useless, pointless life. I wouldn't have to suffer anymore. I wouldn't have to keep feeling the pain. I wouldn't have to keep trudging along even though my life was completely devoid of any meaning whatsoever. This guy had the power to make it all stop. He had the power to take my pain away, forever.

My mind became fixated on ending this. I needed for it all to be over. This horrible experience. My pain. My trauma. My inability to move forward and to enjoy life. The little child who dwells within me simply couldn't continue to exist. There was no way out other than death. I needed to die. There was nothing left for me in this life. Death was my only remaining option. I couldn't do it myself though. Not while I was in handcuffs in police custody. No, I needed Officer Connors to kill me. Suicide by cop.

My thoughts raced. I needed to provoke a lethal confrontation with this officer. All I had to do was attack him, reach for his gun, and hope that he'd panic and shoot me. This was my last option. It was all I could think to do. I was ready to leap forward from my chair when my motivation crumbled beneath me. I was so emotionally broken that I became paralysed. Death by cop? No, the bastards wouldn't even permit me that minor dignity of allowing me to die. They would keep me alive, in prison, purely for spite. I sobbed as I reconsidered, recognizing what a horrible idea I had running through my mind.

Attacking Connors wasn't going to solve anything and I knew it as quickly as that thought had emerged. I would have to wait. I'd have to endure the humiliation at least for a few days. My mind turned to my secondary suicide plan – overdose. At home I had a full bottle of Zoloft. I'd swallow it all and jump from a bridge. There's a large bridge over a river not far from where I live. People have fallen to their deaths there in the past. I knew it was high enough. I knew the river was harsh enough. I knew that Zoloft and alcohol would make me weak enough to succumb to the current beneath those dark, heavy waves.

I was going to do it. I lived in pain for decades. I was haunted by my childhood. A lifetime of depression, anxiety, and persistent existential crisis was more than I could handle.

The encounter with the police forced me to reconsider my entire life. Certain mental barriers were removed and I began to think back on where it all comes from. Where my pain began.

The truth of the matter is that I've never wanted to die. I just want the pain to go away. At that moment I knew that dying wasn't really what I wanted. It was merely a way to stop feeling this pain and torment I've endured almost my entire life. I looked officer Connors in the eyes and in one of my rare moments of honesty I choked out a simple confession: *"I'm going to kill myself."*

It wasn't that I wanted to. It was that I couldn't carry on with this life. Not any longer. Not as someone with an alcohol addiction who was on his way to jail for drunk driving. I couldn't keep living that life. If I had been released that night, the following morning, or whenever I regained my freedom I knew that death awaited me. The scared, emotionally-stunted child inside me knew that I haven't yet reconciled with God. I haven't yet found the forgiveness that

I so desperately need for childhood acts of homosexuality. I still needed more time to find that elusive divine cleansing that my childhood self had quietly sought from the moment that old preacher had condemned me.

I couldn't die without first obtaining God's forgiveness. I long for that forgiveness as crucially as a dehydrated man lost in a desert longs for a glass of water. It is the sustenance my soul has required ever since I was programmed to hate homosexuality.

I looked across the table as a broken shell of a person into the now sympathetic eyes of officer Connors. There I saw something I didn't expect to find – compassion.

That night the police brought me to the psychiatric ward of the hospital rather than jail. I was hurting and I needed help, not punishment. I am forever grateful to officer Connors for that act of compassion and decency. He spared me the indignity of an orange jumpsuit and a further erosion of my own self-identity.

Despite that compassionate gift, I spent that whole night laying awake and wondering if I could hang myself with my shirt and be gone before medical staff would notice. Or if I'd need to wait until I got home to overdose on Zoloft. I cried until my body couldn't produce any more tears. I didn't want to face my family. I was overwhelmed by guilt, shame, and humiliation. It wasn't fair to me. It wasn't fair that I had become an alcohol abuser or that I had lived my life with severe depression and anxiety. It wasn't fair that childhood sexual activities had been used against me by a preacher acting in the name of God to inflict such perilous harm. I was angry. I was sad. I was entirely, completely alone.

There I remained for the night and the full day that followed. That next afternoon while I was still in the psych ward a crisis nurse came to speak with me. The nurse came into the room prepared to break down every last defensive barrier I had maintained to conceal my deepest secrets. She came to find out about my trauma. It was perhaps one of the most important conversations of my life, and it all happened without any warning.

The crisis nurse came into the room and introduced herself and briefly explained a bit about her profession. She asked me about my drinking and if I'd suffered any psychological trauma in my life. I told her about my past, about my drinking, and how I knew that I have some serious issues. I didn't truly want to engage. I didn't want to allow my inner walls to be broken down and to admit to things which I'd kept hidden throughout my life. My secrets were painful and if I let them out, I feared they would overwhelm and destroy me. While we were talking all I could think about was going home to that bottle of Zoloft. I couldn't bear to think of being convicted for drunk driving. My family would be so ashamed and scornful. I never thought I'd be able to face my parents again.

I remained fixated on the imminent crisis before me. The nurse, however, was only interested in my trauma and my addiction. She spent hours talking with me. She asked me about therapy and I replied that I see my therapist, Daryl, often. Without speaking his full name the nurse knew of him immediately. Not only professionally but she also knew a great deal about his private life. Then came a question which truly unsettled me.

"How do you feel discussing these homosexual sexual experiences from your childhood with a gay therapist?" she asked me.

I paused for a moment before I answered. "Are you sure that he's gay?"

"Yes," she answered confidently. "He and his partner have been quite open for several years now."

Of course I had known all along. At least, I had very strongly suspected it. It didn't matter to me in any way. It's just who he is. Though, as I sat with the realization that my therapist had felt the need to conceal his sexual orientation from me I felt a deep sadness. Why did he have to re-closet himself? Why did I have such a difficult time even allowing myself to remember my own past? To allow myself to understand and accept myself? Daryl had lied to me about having a wife named Susan.

I became somewhat angry that I'd been lied to in such a way as it felt a tad bit unethical in the circumstances. Those feelings drifted away rather quickly, though. Then I was left feeling saddened that a gay man had been dealing with me for all those years and that he felt I was so homophobic that he needed to lie to me in order to be able to help me.

I've never told Daryl that I learned the truth. Or that I think what he did was a noble and selfless act which probably came at a cost to his own mental health. A gay man had to sacrifice his own sense of pride and acceptance to not rile the latent homophobia and anger within me. Daryl will never know how much esteem I hold for him, knowing what he did to try to save me from my own destructive ways.

The crisis nurse was adamant that I needed to go to a detox facility and begin treatment for alcohol addiction. I wasn't interested. My emotional state was so low that I didn't have the sense of self-worth to see a value in rehabilitating myself. My life was over. Being charged with drunk driving was too much for me to handle. There was nothing left to rehabilitate. I was gutted. Mentally, I was already gone. To be allowed out of the psych ward, however, I did agree that I would go to the detox treatment center.

I left the hospital without my keys, cell phone, or wallet. The police had held onto all of my personal items, probably to deliberately inconvenience me. I had to walk home from the hospital in the ultimate 'walk of shame' experience. I was still wearing my suit and tie from the wedding. I looked disheveled and hungover. I walked in the hot afternoon sun, drenching myself in sweat. When I arrived home I had to break into my own house. Inside I scraped up some cash and set out to recover my belongings from the police. I wasn't thinking entirely clearly. But I knew I didn't want to leave my possessions with the police. When I got my phone back I had to make the most difficult call of my life.

I had to tell my father — a man who has never once consumed alcohol in his life and who had always instructed me not to drink — that I was charged with drunk driving and that I have an alcohol problem. The disappointment in his voice that day was devastating. He had no idea. None of my family had even suspected that I had a drinking problem. None of them ever thought I would drink and drive. I felt lower than low. I wasn't even human anymore.

I crawled into my bed and I simply shut down. There I remained for hour after hour, day after day. I lost count. I don't know how long I stayed in that room. I know that I had to take a full week away from my job. I simply wasn't able to function. I was a wreck. A spiraling, uncontrollable wreck.

Several days later my father came to see me. He knew that I had fallen apart. I was beaten down and defeated. I'd lost the will even to carry on. It was as if a light inside my heart had burned out and been extinguished. I felt completely gone. There certainly was nothing left inside me even resembling self-respect or a desire to live. Those things were far, far behind me now. I was deeply ashamed even to be seen. I had no right continuing to walk this earth or to breathe this air. I should have been dead, buried, and forgotten.

"I've never seen you just give in before," my father said to me in a somber tone. "You've always been willing to fight. You don't have any fight left in you?"

I didn't. I didn't have any fight left in me. I didn't even have any tears left at this point. He was right. I had no fight left in me. I was done. My pointless life was at its end.

"I can't win," I choked on the words as I spoke barely above a whisper.

My father was so far outside of his element that he didn't know what to say to me. He's a quiet, shy, reserved country boy from a cattle farm. He didn't know what to say to me, nor I to him. I knew that he was hurting though. I knew that I had caused it. He could sense that I had given up entirely. On everything. On being charged with a crime. On life itself. That clearly didn't sit well with him. So he didn't quite push, though there was a bit of a nudge.

We only spoke of defending against the criminal charge. We never spoke about my now apparent alcohol addiction.

"Find a way," my father said softly. "There's always something you didn't know would help you until you look for it."

Chapter 10
Self Defense

To appease my father I agreed to consider defending myself in court. I sat down and wrote detailed notes on everything that had happened the day of my arrest. Every last detail. I documented everything that happened, chronologically, and completely. Then I went looking for similar cases on an online legal database. I didn't have much hope. I mean, I had been driving drunk. I was caught. The police had all the evidence they would need with a breathalyzer report. I really didn't expect to find anything.

To my surprise, after spending a few hours searching for similar court cases I stumbled upon a case just like mine.

The decision was written like a dream. After reading through the entire scenario, which was quite similar to my own circumstances, I got to the judge's decision which may as well have said *"Hey Matt Gordon, I know you are reading this. Use this case as a precedent and you will be free. Free like a bird!"*

It was the perfect case to have me acquitted in court. In that decision a judge determined that if the police decide to involve themselves in contacting a lawyer for an accused person it becomes their responsibility to do everything — *everything* — that a reasonably diligent accused person would do to get into contact with their lawyer of choice. That judge then spelled out using cell phones, obtaining cell phones, finding numbers from other people, using websites, Google searches, lawyer association directories, and the phone book. In my case the police used only an expired phone book. They hadn't done what a reasonable person would do. They hadn't even done the most basic thing that I'd ask them to do.

This case was going to save me. I finally had the ammunition I needed to at least attempt a defense against the criminal charges I was now facing. At least if I could defend myself, I'd have a life worth rebuilding. I wasn't yet ready to tackle the issue of my addiction or my trauma. I was, however, willing to pick myself up off the ground and fight for myself.

I spoke to several lawyers who I know and each of them told me that they don't practice criminal law. None of the lawyers who I knew personally wanted to defend me in court. Part of me knew that they also didn't want to be seen defending a drunk driving case. It was beneath them. I understand that. But with a precedent in my hand which I vehemently believed could be used to have me acquitted, I wasn't going to simply give up and allow a criminal conviction to destroy me.

After finishing my research I phoned up a criminal defense lawyer by the name of Geoff Hubbs. I explained my case to him and then I gave him what I felt was excellent news for a criminal defense lawyer to hear.

"I found the perfect precedent. It clearly spells out that I'm off the hook," I told him.

"Great! Thanks for doing my research for me," he replied sarcastically. "Now I'll be needing a retainer of $10,000," Hubbs said from his second home in, I kid you not, the Cayman Islands. There's something about a criminal defense lawyer living in the Cayman Islands which has a certain cartoonish quality to it. Though, it didn't really matter so long as he could take *and win* my case.

"You need $10,000 for a retainer? I already did all the research," I was shocked by the price tag of my freedom.

"Right. So it would have been $11,000 but I'm giving you a discount," Hubbs was rather transparently mocking me for thinking I had done quality legal research. He was that sort of guy. He didn't care about your feelings. He'd say whatever the hell he wanted if it served his purpose. Exactly the kind of lawyer I needed.

When Hubbs returned from his home in the Caymans we finally met face to face. I presented him with my legal research as well as all of my notes I'd taken from the day of my arrest. After reviewing my documentation, Hubbs was pleasantly surprised. He then asked where I work and how I'm so good at note-taking, writing, and legal research. When I told him where I work Hubbs scoffed before telling me that I am an *"Ambassador from the seventh depth of hell."*

Those were piercing words from a lawyer who suspiciously hangs out offshore most of the time. We didn't have to like each other or become social friends. I just needed him to waltz into court and win. It was that simple.

Hubbs' assistant told me I had drawn judge Andria Horgan. The assistant looked at me for a reaction, while I offered none.

"She's the most difficult judge. This is bad news," the assistant cautioned.

"No way," I thought.

Several years ago Judge Andria Horgan and I locked eyes at a seminar. She smiled. I smiled back. I knew that moment — from many years ago — meant nothing to Andria Horgan. Yet the delusion which I chose to hide behind was that it meant, at first glance, that Andria Horgan at least looked upon me favorably as a person in a neutral setting. Somehow I firmly believed that this meant I had a baseline ability to present myself to this judge in a positive manner. That was a pretty flimsy thought process but somehow it gave me the hefty confidence I would need for my most important personal performance.

I knew that I was going to have to testify in my own defense. And I needed to give a convincing account of how officer Connors stood between me and my constitutionally-guaranteed right to retain and instruct the legal counsel of my choice. It was going to be a battle. I was going to throw everything I could into this fight. I needed to win.

Nothing was too trivial or too ridiculous in this fight for me. Everything possible tactic, down to the clothes I would wear, were up for consideration.

Long before my day in court I took to Google to find out which colors are best to wear in court. Yes, there are plenty of articles on this topic. I learned the following: wear black if you want to offend the judge by being imposing and domineering. Wear red if you're trying to go to jail. Wear yellow if you're an idiot. Wear brown if you're trying to be mistaken for an ugly curtain from the 70s. Or something to that effect. Or, wear light blue if you want to come across as calm, collected, and intelligent. Bingo.

I immediately bought new blue clothes and a blue tie which I'd hoped would convey the subtle message: "I'm too calm and collected to be guilty, your honor."

I was feeling as positive as could be expected with my situation when Hubbs called. Now Hubbs was in a somber mood. He had received the evidence against me and it was difficult to handle. The police had found 2 beers in the trunk of my car that night. A car which was still, months later, sitting in an impound lot. I was devastated. I knew full well there were 10-12 beers back there, so those bastards had clearly stolen my beer. Of course, I jest. The police did in fact steal some of my beer but I wasn't actually going to dwell on that minutiae with so much on the line.

The police had completely contradictory information in their reports from my notes. Officer Connors was swearing up and down that he had used Google and no phone books were ever involved in contacting lawyers on my behalf. According to Connors there isn't even a phone book in the holding area they'd kept me in that night. The police were utterly and completely *lying*.

The cops went further and claimed I was so heavily intoxicated that my face had turned a bright shade of red. The police were lying through their teeth trying to ensure a conviction even if I won some of the smaller tactical legal battles in a court trial.

I told Hubbs that I remembered every last thing about that phone book. Most notably, that it had expired. It had writing all over it. It was worn out. It was a shade of yellow. I had every last detail. Still, Hubbs wasn't convinced. He thought, somehow, I must be wrong. Or lying. Or both. My lawyer was beginning to doubt me as well as my ability to persuade judge Horgan.

Luckily, the police then inadvertently gave me a chance to prove my own side of the story. Throughout the many months between my arrest and my court trial the police acted as though I'd already been found guilty. They had towed my car to an impound lot and refused to let anyone drive it out of there for me. They confiscated my driver's license to prevent me from driving any other vehicle. Before I'd even had my day in court and without being found guilty by a judge. The police were just seizing anything they could from me, the laws of this country be damned.

Continuing their campaign against me, the police then summoned me back to the police station to be fingerprinted, photographed, and added to a database of convicted criminals. This wasn't contingent upon having my day in court and being found guilty. No, they wanted to add all of this information into a database of convicted criminals *before* my trial. The presumption of innocence is a concept lost on the local constabulary.

The police actually scheduled my fingerprinting for an hour before my first appearance in court, which was on the other side of town. They were trying to make me miss one of those two 'required' appearances. Or at the very least, they were trying to give me a nervous breakdown.

I put on a suit and tie and took a taxi to the police station. Of course I had to take a taxi. They'd seized my driver license and impounded my car for months on end. I walked in there with every intention of being the most polite, calm, and courteous person they dealt with that day. I had to act this way because I had a hidden agenda with my visit to the police station. My goal was to obtain photos of their phone books. The phonebook officer Connors was now pretending didn't actually exist.

Luck was finally on my side for a change. Connors wasn't there that day. A beautiful blonde female cop was assigned to take my fingerprints and photos. After smiling, conversing, and generally behaving as a friendly and respectable citizen, that female officer came to believe that she could leave me unsupervised for a brief moment. It was everything I needed to conduct my own miniature espionage operation.

In the mere minutes she left me alone I was able to stroll into the holding area and locate the exact phone book officer Connors had used the night of my arrest. I took several photos of the phone book he now claimed didn't exist. I had close-up photos of the book and photos of the entire interrogation room. Exactly what I had sought out to obtain.

With only a second or two to spare I darted back to where the female officer had left me. She had no idea I'd stepped away or taken any photos. It was a perfect success for me. I had the evidence I needed without anyone ever knowing I'd collected the proof. Might I add that I had acquired these photos entirely lawfully. After all, I was in the police station at their very formal invitation that day. They never asked me to leave my camera at home.

I spent that entire summer reliving my DUI. I read my notes of the incident every single day. I wasn't going to trip up on the stand. I was going to know every last detail, no matter how insignificant. I invested countless hours in ensuring I knew exactly what to say and what not to say when I would testify in court. I thought about it every day, afternoon, and night. I lived it. I breathed it.

My court date was the only thing that mattered in my life that summer. The court trial dwelled so vociferously within my mind that my hairline started to recede. Each morning I would wake up to find dozens upon dozens of hairs had fallen from atop my head. The stress was taking a physical toll on me. I had no choice but to continue until this battle was over.

Beginning to lose my hair, though, was a cruel expense. I so very much loved the way women always admired my hair. It was something I never thought about myself until woman after woman would tell me how 'perfect' my hair was. It was a welcomed compliment for a guy who had virtually no real self-esteem to speak of. I'd never worried about going bald before, but I now found myself having nightmares almost every night in which I'd lost all or huge swaths of my hair. It may seem vain to some. My hair was really the one thing I had going for me in this life. That DUI charge took it from me and my physical appearance aged 5 years or more in the span of 5 months.

Having collected the photos of the police interrogation room phone book, I showed my lawyer the proof I'd collected and watched as his whole outlook on the case shifted. I realized that he didn't think I had an ice cube's chance in hell of being acquitted, until I showed him those photos. That's when he finally got on board and truly believed that everything that I was saying was true. Still, though, this wasn't going to be court checkers — this was court 3D chess. I had to navigate not only the facts and realities of the case from the witness stand but also the landmine lies the police were laying for me.

Hubbs warned me that in a 'credibility contest' between the cops and the accused judges side with the cops every time. In this case, we had clear evidence that the cops were lying in their testimony. They were luring me into a credibility contest with the false bravado that they would ultimately win. They were telling frivolous lies so that I would attempt to refute each of their little lies, creating an ever-expanding cleavage between their version of events and mine. They hoped to win a credibility contest by default.

Challenge accepted.

Every sunny day for weeks leading up to the trial I spent every possible minute in direct sunlight. I deliberately sunburned my face the day before my trial. My logic was simple. I'd learned through my research that the police had lied about me having a 'red face' on the night of my arrest so that they could fall back on that 'evidence' to prove I was drunk while driving in case the breathalyzer report was thrown out of court as inadmissible evidence. If they were going to argue that a red face was proof of being drunk, my best rebuttal was to show up as red as a lobster while as sober as a Mississippi Sunday school teacher.

When I explained my sunburn to Hubbs he laughed at me and asked "So you'd rather have skin cancer than a criminal record?"

The answer was an obvious 'yes.' I had done everything I could to prepare for this trial. Finally, the day had arrived.

Chapter 11
Judgment Day

Sitting just outside the courtroom on the day of my trial I heard someone loudly complaining about getting stuck with a case at the last minute. There was nothing else going on around me. It was just a large waiting area and this was the only source of noise for my ears to focus upon. Naturally, I could do nothing but hear what was being spoken. The woman continued to rant. Apparently her office stuck her with a case with only a weekend to prepare for trial. The woman loudly announced her intention to play games to obstruct the trial in an effort to buy herself more time to prepare. Which trial was she planning to obstruct? Oh, that would be *mine*.

My lawyer and I sat listening to the prosecutor standing in the foyer outside the courtroom pronouncing her intention to play procedural games to prevent the trial from happening that day because she wasn't ready.

"Hubbs, she seems like a bit of an idiot to be shouting that for anyone to hear," I whispered.

"She might be the winning factor for you," Hubbs smiled. "She's absolutely off the wall. She drives Judge Horgan crazy. She will annoy everyone in that courtroom so much that it will be *her* on trial instead of you."

"Let's do this, Hubbs," I said to him as we rose to our feet to walk toward the biggest battle of my life.

I truly mean that. In many ways it was the most difficult day of my life. My very freedom was on the line. If I lost I was going to jail. I'd lose my license, my reputation, my job, and my self-respect. There was so much on the line that I couldn't afford the slightest gaffe or misstep. Nothing on that day was going to come easily, either.

I was wearing a full cotton suit on a record-breaking day that was both hotter and more humid than anything my city had seen for five years. My face was lobster-red with a sunburn. Part of my strategy was that I had to be a perfect gentleman the entire day. Every facial movement, every gesture, every placement of the arm. It all had to be artfully choreographed for the judge's viewing pleasure. I needed her to see a positive image of a good person — *an innocent person.*

Sitting down at the defense table I pulled out a notebook and pen. I started taking notes that I knew I would never, ever need. Why? Because my research told me it's an effective psychological tactic which conveys to the judge that you're preparing for an appeal if the decision doesn't come in your favor. Judges hate having their decisions overturned. It was a harmless tactic on my part which may or may not have tipped the scales slightly in my favor. Though, it was a total bluff because I had completely run out of money. I had to borrow everything that I could to pay my lawyer for this trial. There was no chance whatsoever that I could pay for an appeal if things didn't work out.

As Judge Horgan began the proceeding the prosecutor immediately launched an objection. It was a scene right out of a Hollywood movie. The prosecutor was demanding Hubbs call me as a witness and present his evidence. This was about thirty seconds into the trial. The judge hadn't even gotten to 'good morning' yet in her opening remarks. Naturally, Judge Horgan looked totally confused.

Hubbs had no idea what had just happened. Even though we knew the prosecutor planned to play games it still came as a surprise when she resorted to such bizarre theatrics. I suppose we had at least been expecting her tactics to lead toward her desired outcome of delaying the trial. What she attempted right out of the gate in no way served her own objective, as we understood it.

Judge Horgan seemed annoyed that she had to explain to the prosecutor that *she* is the one attempting to prosecute *me* and that I was presumed innocent until proven guilty. If no arguments were made against me it simply didn't make sense for my lawyer to stand up and start speaking. I was already innocent by default and it was the prosecutor's job to change that. It was an embarrassing and awkward display. As the only person who could benefit from the prosecutor's buffoonery I struggled to remain composed as the prosecutor basically then challenged Judge Horgan that the trial is not in fact *a trial*.

Yes, that really happened. And yes I had to sit there with a straight face throughout all of it.

The prosecutor tried to argue that the only item up for consideration that day was a "pretrial motion" and that the trial was, at least in her imagination, scheduled for some future point in time. Of course there hadn't been a pretrial motion and the trial was most certainly scheduled for this very date and this very time in this very courtroom. These antics went on for over 45 minutes before the judge had finally had enough of the prosecution's shenanigans. Judge Horgan made clear in very simple terms that either the prosecutor engaged in an attempt to prosecute me for my alleged crime or I was being sent on my merry way. If only I had been so lucky.

I consider myself to be a very astute judge of character. I can usually size a person up quite quickly. I stared into the prosecutor's soul and arrived at a clear conclusion: I can not only defeat her in a battle of wits but it would be embarrassing how easily I could outmaneuver her.

I turned to my lawyer and whispered: "Hubbs, if she wants us to go first. Let's go first."

"Let's do it!" Hubbs answered. He quickly rose to his feet and offered to the judge that we would present our defense right off the bat, essentially out of politeness.

It was an amazing tactic. We looked like heroic nice guys getting this trial back on track. Of course, we had the benefit of knowing from her own foolish blathering in the foyer that the prosecutor wasn't ready for a trial yet. Salvaging that trial date ensured we were up against a prosecutor who simply wasn't up to speed and hadn't prepared her arguments in advance.

We had the opportunity to square off against an unarmed opponent who didn't know the case and who hadn't done her homework. We couldn't let that opportunity slip away. We jumped to our feet and pressed the judge to keep the trial going. It gave me a huge psychological boost to know that I was fully prepared while the prosecutor was not. That was a genuine confidence which I needed to keep myself going.

I was immediately called to the stand where my own lawyer tossed softball questions at me. Hubbs just asked the basics. 'What happened? When did it happen? Did they let you speak with your lawyer?'

I was the one telling the story. I was shaping the narrative of the whole event. Getting to speak first, actually, seemed like a huge advantage. At least that's how it felt to me.

It didn't take the prosecutor very long before she realized this trial was totally beyond her control and that she was off to a terrible start.

"Objection!" the prosecutor shouted.

Judge Horgan glared while waiting for an explanation of the nature of objection.

The prosecutor just stared back, apparently lacking in the knowledge that she must explain the nature of her objection. An awkward pause ensued. Judge Horgan then demanded the prosecutor explain herself. The prosecutor launched into a philosophical debate about the nature of court trials. She was unhappy. She felt things weren't going as planned, at least according to her own plan. She felt like everyone was against her. It just wasn't fair to her. She wanted the judge to explain to her what she needed to prove to win the case because she didn't quite understand the burden of proof.

It was like being prosecuted by someone who wasn't even a lawyer but who had just shown up to the court that day and decided to try out the role of prosecutor to see if it was a good fit. And it wasn't a good fit, not that I had any complaints.

Judge Horgan explained that it would be helpful to the prosecutor's case if she proved that I had actually committed the crime of drunk driving and that the police had properly investigated and charged me in accordance with the law and my rights as a citizen. The prosecutor, in response, felt that was unfair. She then admitted that this wasn't even her case. She was just filling in for another prosecutor. The prosecutor elaborated that she didn't think she should have to prove that the police had acted in accordance with law. She only wanted to prove that I had been drunk while driving and that the process by which the police gathered their evidence was irrelevant.

The judge angrily shouted at the prosecutor to "sit down."

The trial was clearly going in my favor. Hubbs' prediction was coming to fruition: the prosecutor was so ill-prepared and uncouth that she had put herself on trial, not me. But we were getting ever-closer to something I'd been lamenting for months at this point. Hubbs had warned me dozens of times that the first thing "a smart prosecutor" would ask me is how much alcohol I had consumed that night. He said just by asking the question I would lose. The judge would look at me, see me squirm in embarrassment and shame, and know that I had been drinking. That would be it. A judge would just hold onto that moment throughout the trial and somehow find me guilty, Hubbs said.

He had warned me over and over that I cannot lie on the stand. About anything. Not one little lie.

Yet, the truth to that question would have me thrown into prison.

"How much alcohol did you consume that night?" The thought of that question haunted me. It made my stomach twist and knot. I couldn't answer with a lie; I couldn't bear to speak the truth.

The moment of reckoning was finally upon me. The prosecutor stood to ask her first question. She looked straight into my eyes and began: "Mr. Gordon. You have testified here today that you spoke with a lawyer for 90 minutes that night, right?"

I could have fallen out of my chair. I was awe-struck by her question. It was nothing close to what Hubbs had told me to expect. She wasn't asking how much I drank that night. She wasn't asking me about alcohol at all. I'm not even sure she was asking a question that pertained even to my trial. I had not said anything even close to what she had asked me.

Confused, I replied that she was incorrect. She tried again: "Mr. Gordon, is it not true that you lied here today?"

It was an outlandishly awkward question. What made it worse was the tone of voice she had used. It was like hearing Caitlin Upton's confused beauty pageant commentary about *'South Africa and the Iraq and the places such as. For the children.'*

This prosecutor sounded totally confused, inept, and clueless! She had only briefly skimmed a few pages of the file presented to her by the police and her own office. She vaguely knew that me speaking to a lawyer that night was a point of contention, but that seemed to be all she knew. Without having done her pre-trial homework, the prosecutor just asked me if I was lying and hoped that I would come back with *"Ya got me! I confess! And I killed the Lindbergh baby, too!"*

I wasn't about to just surrender on the stand seemingly for no reason.

"No," I answered unequivocally. "I haven't lied."

The prosecutor's line of questioning never recovered. She simply hadn't read the file before arriving in court that morning and had no clue as to what to say or where to go with her line of questioning. After floundering for 15 minutes or so she asked the judge for a much-needed recess to gather her thoughts.

While I thought everything was going incredibly well for me, Hubbs had an entirely different perspective when we convened outside the courtroom.

"What is it with you young pretty-boy conservative types always trying to make everyone fall in love with you?" Hubbs chirped. "You aren't here to make friends. You're here to get your life back. Answer her stupid questions. Stop being a politician."

At first, I didn't know what it was that he was so upset about. I thought for sure I was winning hands down. Then I recalled something Hubbs had taught me when we were preparing for the trial. He asked me *"Do you know what time it is?"* and I answered by telling him the time.

"No," he shook his head. "I asked you *if you know the time.*"

I had been somewhat puzzled for a brief moment before he explained "the answer is either a 'yes' or a 'no.' Don't volunteer any more than that."

While I felt entirely confident that I was winning on the stand, Hubbs wasn't impressed with my performance. He felt that I was trying to do more than simply answer the questions posed to me, which was an unnecessary risk. He was right. I had been trying to make the judge like me, which was the wrong approach. I was only supposed to present my story about the police standing between me and my lawyer of choice, answer questions, and get out of the witness stand unscathed.

Hubbs would take care of the rest. It didn't matter if the judge liked me. She just needed to believe that officer Connors had impeded me from contacting the lawyer of my choice. That's it. That was the whole defense. Because if the judge believed that, all evidence collected after that point in time was inadmissible.

In this trial, the only real evidence was the breathalyzer report. Which is evidence collected *after* my right to retain and instruct the legal counsel of my choice had been impeded by officer Connors. No breathalyzer report would mean they have no evidence Mr. Lobsterface here had been driving drunk.

After the recess the prosecutor came at me again. This time it was clear that she had at least spoken to the police about the case and had a rudimentary understanding of how it all unfolded.

"Mr. Gordon, isn't it true that when you told officer Connors your lawyer's name you called him *James Mark* instead of *Mark James?*" she asked smugly, as if the question itself was fatal to my defense.

This question had come from officer Connors who had been silently sitting in the courtroom watching the prosecutor's trainwreck performance and apparently decided to help out. The only problem is that Connors was completely misremembering the night of my arrest. Unlike me, Connors didn't have the benefit of reading detailed notes each and every day from the time of the arrest until the day of the trial.

He had other people to prosecute. I only had one trial to worry about. It was his memory that was faulty, not mine.

Still on the witness stand, I actually chuckled at the question. I've been friends with Mark James since 2002. We go to the same gym and every year we volunteer for the same organization to clean up local hiking trails. He's in the same social circles I am. Of course I know his name. It was such a ridiculous question that I literally let out an unguarded chuckle on the stand.

"No! That is not correct at all. I told officer Connors that Mark James is programmed into the contacts list in my phone as *"James, Mark"* and asked him to use my phone to get Mark's number. I had been telling him this because that's how easy it would have been to allow me to contact my own lawyer that night." My answer was genuine, honest, and one-hundred percent true.

Officer Connors no doubt remembered the brief exchange and desperately tried to use it against me, months later, after he himself misremembered.

I watched officer Connors, the prosecutor, and all of the other prosecutorial staff assembled in the courtroom deflated like used birthday balloons. They'd tried to make it look like I was so drunk I couldn't even give my lawyer's name. No doubt, they would argue that this is why the police took charge of contacting a lawyer for me. But the flawlessly honest and immediate response that I'd given showed everyone in that courtroom that I had a clear working memory of everything that had happened that night. How could my memory be so clear all those months later if I'd been drunk at the time?

Judge Horgan actually looked amused with the way the trial was going. I could sense her feeling that I was being honest. Indeed, I *was* being honest. The truth always comes out more naturally and easily than a lie. I knew that the judge had detected and took note of my honest and sincere reply. That question had been an enormous gift to me.

The prosecutor knew she was losing so she changed tack and hurled a quick series of questions at me. Hubbs objected to each of them. The prosecutor then pleaded with the judge saying: "I'm allowed to ask leading questions to see if he will agree!"

Judge Horgan scolded the prosecutor that she isn't allowed to present falsehoods as facts and then vocalize a question mark at the end of her sentence just to see what I will say. Which is exactly what the prosecutor had attempted.

Rebuked once more by the judge, she sank into her chair almost ready to accept defeat.

Finally, the judge handed things back to Hubbs. Hubbs asked the court staff to turn on a TV sitting off to the side of the room. Everyone at the prosecutor's table looked uneasy and apprehensive. If they'd read the files sitting on the desk before them, surely they'd have known what Hubbs was about to broadcast to the court.

There on the 65-inch TV was photo after photo of the now infamous phone book the police insisted did not exist. Hubbs asked me to describe the evidence on the screen as the police officers and prosecutors did double-takes looking at the photos. Here was the phone book the police claimed they hadn't used. They claimed it didn't even exist. They swore in their written testimony that they had used Google to contact my lawyer. This phone book spoke to my credibility and theirs. I said it existed. They said it didn't. Now it's on screen as Exhibit X in court evidence.

Every single cop in the court looked as guilty as a four year old next to spilled grape juice all over grandma's couch.

'Yup. I have proof of your ancient phone book,' I smugly thought on the witness stand.

Judge Horgan turned to the prosecutor. "Anything to say with respect to this evidence?" she asked.

There was a momentary pause before the prosecutor could muster any kind of a response.

"No," she eventually answered in half the decibels she had been using throughout the trial.

I was done answering questions on the stand. I felt like I held my own. I punched above my weight. I was winning. I sauntered off the witness stand like a champ. I sat down beside Hubbs and went back into perfect gentleman mode. Arms where they belong. Facial expressions contained. Eyes focussed straight toward the judge. All I had to do was hold that stoic posture and wait for Hubbs to tear officer Connors apart on the stand.

I had mixed emotions as I watched Connors move into the box where I'd been sitting all morning. After all, he had shown me compassion that night. I considered him to be a nice person. He was only doing his job. I didn't want to see him humiliated or lose face. He didn't deserve that. Though, it was the only way to guarantee my freedom.

It was now officer Connors' turn on the stand. I had no way of knowing how this would go. I was worried he'd somehow find a way to sink me even though, so far, Hubbs and I had done an effective job of proving to the judge that the police had actually violated my right to retain a lawyer prior to collecting a breathalyzer sample.

Unless Connors could torpedo me with his testimony somehow, I should be walking out of this courtroom a free man when this is over.

It seems my good fortune for the day had not yet run dry. I sat in disbelief as the prosecutor asked officer Connors a series of questions that could only possibly help me. Connors even admitted that he knew I had my cell phone with me that night with the cell phone number for my lawyer. He knew that my lawyer wouldn't be working at the office that late on a weekend night. He knew that lawyers don't put their cell phone numbers into the Yellow Pages. He knew that he wasn't supposed to interfere with an arrested person trying to call their lawyer. Connors actually confirmed that I had been telling the truth all along in my witness testimony.

Connors even made the laughable comment that after he'd decided to arrest me for drunk driving that he asked me to pull my car forward and off to the shoulder of the road.

Hubbs stood up to ask: "Officer Connors, you say you believe my client was impaired. But then you asked him to drive his vehicle forward and park on the shoulder of the road? Why would you ask an impaired person to operate a motor vehicle?" Connors didn't have much of an answer to that other than to suggest that I wasn't all that drunk. Perhaps not even intoxicated at all!

Officer Connors may as well have been testifying for the defense because his every comment helped me, rather than served to convict me.

In the end the judge determined that the police had violated my constitutional right to contact my lawyer after I had been accused of a crime. As a result, any evidence collected after that point in time was deemed inadmissible in court. The only actual evidence the police had against me was the breathalyzer report which was now just a sheet of paper sitting in a waste bin someplace as far as the court was concerned. I was off the hook. I was free.

When the trial concluded I turned to Hubbs, politely shook his hand while Judge Horgan watched on with a genuine curiosity. I know that in the back of her mind she knew I had been over the legal limit that night. Although the breathalyzer report had never been brought into the court as admissible evidence, it obviously existed and it obviously indicated something which led the police to charge me with the crime of drunk driving. She knew all of that. I was still walking away from court that day as a free, innocent person.

I could have my life back. I had my freedom. I had my second chance. I had everything God told me would happen that night in the car. I was free – and now it's up to me to make something better of myself.

It's time for me to get sober. It's time for me to heal from the trauma that brought me there.

***

Defending myself in court cost me $10,000 in legal fees. My car had been impounded by the police for months. They charged me $3,000 in impound fees to get my car back. I'd started to lose my hair. The police in my hometown now have a grudge against me and I've been warned that they'll retaliate against me when they get the chance.

Psychologically, I endured a daily and continuous stress which lasted several months from the date of my arrest until the date I was acquitted in court. It was an enormous ordeal which changed my life forever.

I will never be so foolish, reckless, or selfish ever again. I will not drink and drive. I will become that good person I was always meant to be. I recognize that it was a constitutional technicality which saved me in that courtroom that day. I owe it to myself and to all of society to make the most of my second chance in life and to be a better person tomorrow than I have been in my past.

Chapter 12
Detox

I sat outside on my patio with the sun warming my face. I only had one day left in my life as an alcohol abuser. Only one more day and then I'd be a changed person. It was the day before I went to detox. One last opportunity to drink some of my favorite beers. It made me sad to think that I could never have a beer or a glass of wine again. There are so many beers and wines which I love. How can I just never experience that again? How can I honestly commit in my thirties to never having another alcoholic beverage? It's unfathomable. Certainly, before I'd been to treatment, it was absolutely ridiculous to think that I could just never drink again. I tried not to think about it too much and I went to pick up some of my favorites from the liquor store.

I honestly didn't know what to expect or what to think. But just in case I found myself in a world where I could never drink again I wanted to have one last hurrah with the only friend I have left: *alcohol.*

I had a lot of thinking to do so I went for a long drive out in the country. Not too far from home, but I was far enough away that I landed in a liquor store I hadn't gone to in many years. I didn't think much of it. I grabbed some craft beers, some imported beers, and a 4-pack of one of my favorite India Pale Ales. I was going to have an assortment of flavors and, perhaps unsurprisingly, I was very much looking forward to it. I walked up to the checkout. When I got to the cash I realized that I vaguely recognized the cashier. That struck me as odd given that I was a fair distance away from my usual neck of the woods. I looked at his nametag and immediately realized how I know him.

It was the man whose wife I'd had an affair with. The man whose wife I had impregnated. The man I had been so awful toward years ago. He smiled at me, totally unaware of who I was. I carried on like there was nothing to it. Like there was nothing meaningful about that moment. Even though I knew there was something fateful about this interaction. I don't know if I'll ever forget the smile on his face. He seemed like a happy, genuinely nice guy. And what was I? The jackass alcohol abuser who ruined his marriage.

I didn't feel cocky about it this time. I wasn't happy and pleased with myself for sleeping with his wife, thinking that I was better than him, as I had before. There was nothing to be proud of at that moment. The only thought that I had was that he was a genuinely good person who I had hurt for no reason.

I suppose he'll never know that I wrote these words or the fulsome sincerity with which I utter them. I am forever sorry for that pain and hurt that I caused. I am forever sorry that I masked my own issues and challenges by bringing heartache and suffering to other people. I'm sorry for what I did. I am ashamed of my behavior and I hope to leave this world as a better person than how I had lived throughout those years.

The next morning I packed my bag and I went to detox. I told my family that I was going to "a hospital for a medical treatment." I said that I would be gone for several days but that I didn't want to talk about my medical issue. I took a week of vacation from work. For something that was such a major event in my life it's incredible how simplistic it all sounds upon reflection. It was as simple as just taking the time and going to where I needed to go. Yet I had found a thousand excuses not to take that time and not to go to that place for a decade.

All that lost time. All those missed opportunities for happiness. I truly wish I had seen the light years sooner. But I am thankful to have seen it at all.

I've been living in fear of prisons, confined spaces, forced social interactions, and sobriety. I was terrified to go to detox. I was scared that I would cry in front of other people. I was scared that I'd be sick, running to the bathroom with diarrhea from withdrawal, and sweating profusely. I didn't want to admit this to anyone at the time but I was also scared that I just wouldn't be able to socialize properly. Through it all, I am still emotionally-scarred and unable to control the anger, sadness, and rage which sometimes rises to the surface without warning.

Detox was my worst nightmare. Until I actually got there. At first it was difficult and dehumanizing. They asked me to strip down, which I found awkward. They asked me for my whole history of substance use right away which had me breaking down in tears. It was a huge psychological mountain to climb. That first day they basically brought me to my room and told me to lay down and let them know when the withdrawal started. So that's all I did. I laid there for a few hours until I started to panic and experience the initial signs of withdrawal. I told a nurse when the withdrawal started and she casually handed me a Valium.

After struggling with alcohol abuse and addiction for 12 years it just seems so simplistic to me now. But that's all there was to it. The nurse handed me a Valium. So I was fine. No more crying. No getting sick. No sweating. No heart palpitations. None of that. I just laid down on the bed and waited. Later that night they came and gave me a sleeping pill. I drifted off to sleep, leaving my days of rampant alcoholism behind me.

My second day in detox I met with the doctor. He asked me if I'd experienced any trauma in my life. I was able to be honest with him, which was very difficult for me and took a great deal of mental clarity. I told him about my childhood same-sex experiences. I told him how this significantly impacted my sexual identity and my belief system. I told him about self-harm behaviors.

These are things which have haunted me throughout my life. I've kept some of these secrets from everyone, for nearly 25 years. I was finally able to just let it all out and I did it all in less than ten minutes.

The doctor ran through an 'alcohol abuse disorder' checklist with me. He told me that I hit 11 out of 11 indicators for alcohol abuse disorder, following that up by saying that most people with alcohol abuse disorders would usually only hit 5 or 6. He told me that he was going to prescribe Naltrexone. I almost pushed back because of my long history of side-effects from pharmaceuticals. The doctor actually only discussed Naltrexone with me for a minute or so. He said I'd be taking it every day for 6 months. That it would decrease my desire to drink. If I did drink I wouldn't enjoy drinking so I would drink less.

It all sounded so simple. I thought for sure this new drug must have terrible side effects.
I asked if it was anything like Antabuse and he quickly told me it was nothing like Antabuse. He said it wouldn't make me sick if I did drink. He followed that up by saying 'Naltrexone is lightyears ahead of Antabuse.' With that he wished me well and told me that I was going to be much better off with Naltrexone.

I was in detox for only four days. During that time I went from being the one guy who didn't talk to anyone else, who sat alone during meals, to seeing the progression in myself and those around me. Everyone went through the same experience. The first day they hide in their room in their bed. The second day they come out a little bit, but run back to their room after minor interactions. The third day you're out talking with other people who are going through the exact same thing you are. After four days I was fine.

That was detox. I only needed 3 Valium pills the entire time. I took sleeping pills and I just didn't have any access to alcohol. That was it. I was released into the world, sober, ready to improve my quality of life and equipped with a new prescription which I couldn't wait to run home and Google. I was convinced the doctor had downplayed any negative side effects of the drug. How completely wrong I was about something which undoubtedly saved my life.

I have only one thing to say to those who are struggling with alcohol: *the Sinclair Method.* Google it.

Chapter 13
Naltrexone

In my area there is a head doctor who deals with addictions.
When I was in detox he prescribed Naltrexone 50mg tablets
for daily use for 6 months. The doctor described it as being a
medication which would reduce my cravings for alcohol and
if I did slip up and drink it would block an endorphin release,
thereby dissuading me from continuing to drink. Neither my
mental health therapist nor my addictions counselor had any
experience with Naltrexone. People I'd met through AA
hadn't heard of it either. My pharmacist was about the only
person I could speak to about Naltrexone. He was curious
about why I was taking the medication daily. When I was
picking up the prescription for the first time the pharmacist
told me to go home and Google 'The Sinclair Method.' He
said that he suspects this is what the doctor intended for me
to be doing.

My experiences with Naltrexone are surely not the norm. My
body simply doesn't adjust well to pharmaceuticals.
Naltrexone gave me instant and severe headaches, extreme

exhaustion, insomnia, and a constant need for more water. After a month of daily use of Naltrexone, something had to give. I'd tried tinkering with the time of day when I take the pill or taking only half the tablet. A few times I didn't take Naltrexone at all just to confirm the symptoms were caused by the medication and not post acute withdrawal. It was the Naltrexone causing those side effects. There's no question.

Though, it works. Naltrexone, in my experience, absolutely works. It dramatically reduces my desire to drink. I feel physically and psychologically different about 30 minutes after taking a Naltrexone tablet. It works. So I'm determined to continue using this prescription to support my recovery, despite the side effects.

Naltrexone doesn't seem to have this impact on others, but it hits me like a heavy dose of sleeping pills leaving a lingering confusion for about 12-18 hours after consumption. I can't spend 6 months of my life totally exhausted, loopy, and confused. There's simply not an option, yet the benefits from Naltrexone are clear and compelling. Recognizing both of these realities I began to focus more and more on what my pharmacist had suggested: the Sinclair Method.

Because of the way my doctor had described Naltrexone I felt that drinking while taking the medication was essentially a relapse. It wasn't something to be encouraged, but would be viewed as a failure in my recovery. Imagine my surprise then when I found article after article and video after video of people telling me that I'm supposed to drink alcohol while taking Naltrexone. It didn't seem right. In fact, it seemed like a bunch of alcohol abusers in denial had convinced themselves and were now attempting to persuade others that it's okay to keep drinking even though you're an abuser of alcohol.

I watched a Ted Talk with Claudia Christian discussing the Sinclair Method, which she and others commonly abbreviate to 'TSM'. When she described herself and her struggles with alcohol I strongly identified with her experiences and her reactions to things such as seeing an advertisement for wine. She's lived my struggle. I recognize it when I hear it. The sincerity in her hurt, her pain, her frustration, and her hope — all if it was so genuine and familiar. I heard myself in her words. But I still wasn't convinced.

After all, I'd been working on my longest period of sobriety in my life. Hearing someone tell me I'm supposed to pick up a drink again seemed fundamentally wrong. I very much appreciated Claudia Christian's message but I didn't think 'TSM' was for me. It sounded like Plan B for those who hadn't been able to achieve sobriety. Still, my curiosity lingered.

As the days and weeks went on I knew that Naltrexone was a major component to my health and recovery. While at the same time I knew that daily use of Naltrexone isn't going to work over the long term. I continued to research the drug searching for more information or answers on how I can keep this highly beneficial piece in place in support of my long-term recovery. This led me to a YouTube channel for Katie Lain. Katie is a beautiful young blonde with a soothing voice. I didn't realize she actually makes videos regularly, at first, I just thought she was a regular person sharing a part of her story.

Listening to Katie I was again struck by how much I identified with her story. At one point I stopped multi-tasking and just focussed on Katie's face while she spoke. I looked into her eyes and felt, again, that I was listening to a sincere, genuine, and honest person sharing a story which was so much like my own. Katie described being able to drink socially a few times a month without getting drunk and without feeling that uncontrollable urge, or compulsion to over-indulge. I was fascinated by what she was describing but still I didn't think it was possible. One drink, I thought, and everything would fall apart for me.

Days later my interest in Naltrexone brought me to a video of Katie interviewing Samantha Ferris. I turned the video on while I went about cleaning my house. I was in and out of several rooms and wasn't really paying attention to the faces or voices, only the message. Something about Samantha Ferris seemed familiar to me but by this point it seemed likely that I was just identifying with her experience and her alcohol use. After a time I stopped and stared at the TV. I immediately recognized Samantha Ferris as an actress who played a role in one of my all-time favorite TV shows, The 4400.

I'd begun watching The 4400 right around the time I'd started drinking heavily. Hearing an actress from a show I had so loved all those years ago really struck me. So I sat down and gave the video my undivided attention.

Call me skeptical or cynical or just plain negative. Something about all of these people espousing the Sinclair Method just seemed off to me. I felt like people were trying to sell something to me. It seemed like an excuse to keep drinking.

How could continuing to drink alcohol possibly be of any benefit whatsoever to me after achieving a month of sobriety? This was either just some other religion for alcohol abusers, a multi-level marketing scheme about asking me for money, or people who are so far down with their head in the sand that they can't be heard in a rational world.

I was sure of it. They're wrong. They're advancing a message I've never heard before. They're talking about one of society's biggest and most damaging problems. And they're just casually suggesting that there's what I would call a cure to this problem. They may as well have been telling me that the ancient Egyptians exchanged ambassadors with alien civilizations because what they're all saying is of such a magnitude that it defies belief that they could be right.

Still, they had my attention. That weekend I had to attend an event where everyone would be drinking alcohol. I'd tried to get out of it. I tried to delay the event. I'd tried everything I could short of just admitting to my fragile sobriety and continuous cravings. There was no way out, I had to go. Worse, the alcohol would be free. I couldn't even leave my wallet at home and pretend that I just can't buy a beer or a glass of wine. It was free. They'd just hand it to me and wait for me to trade an empty glass for another. I felt embarrassed. I knew that I was in a dangerous situation and that I didn't have the coping skills or the defenses yet to survive such an event.

Before going to the event I read through a scientific study on Naltrexone. The findings were clear: if you drink on Naltrexone you can unlearn alcohol addiction and become a 'regular' person when it comes to alcoholic beverages. The study directly concluded that using Naltrexone daily without consuming alcohol is not as effective as, essentially, the Sinclair Method. I decided to try it.

At my event I had 4 beers over the span of four and a half hours. I'll admit, that's twice as much as I intended to drink. I told myself I'd only have 2. That being said, 4 beers at a large social gathering which lasted for hours is the smallest amount of alcohol I've ever had in such circumstances. Normally I'd have had 4 or 5 beers before I arrived and been continuously guzzling drinks the entire time. Only two months ago if I'd gone to the same event there's no question it would have been a 15-drink kind of night. Not only did Naltrexone dramatically reduce how much I drank but I can honestly say that I was perfectly content the entire time. I didn't have an urge to drink more. I wasn't desperately trying to get drunk. I was having a sip every so often at the same pace as those around me.

Naltrexone is my cure for alcohol use disorder, alcoholism, being a total boozebag — whatever terminology you want to use is fine. My point is simple: Naltrexone is a cure, in my view, for alcohol addiction. How nobody seems to know about this drug and the Sinclair Method is not only a mystery to me but it's an absolute travesty. If you or someone you love is struggling with alcohol abuse disorder, please research Naltrexone and the Sinclair Method and speak with a qualified medical practitioner.

Chapter 14
Understanding Conversion Therapy

I was deeply uncomfortable when I first learned of a political push to legislatively ban 'conversion therapy.' I was deeply angry at the thought of such a ban. It sounded to me as though political extremists were seeking to pass a law prohibiting mental health professionals from giving treatment to people like me. Because on some level I knew that being counseled toward straightness was something that I would want. It was something that I craved. I needed some guidance and help to get myself from where I was to the happy, mentally-healthy, straight person I wanted to be.

All I want is to be like everyone else. I want to be happy and to be able to live in peace with myself, my past, and my present. I want to allow the secrets and the tension to leave my body. I want to have normal sexual preferences and desires, which are the same or at least mostly similar to what everyone else desires.

Banning conversion therapy sounded worringly close to passing a law that says therapists can't help a person like me to work through my past and have them reassure me that I'm straight. I wanted that reassurance. I needed to have someone listen to my heart and soul and tell me that I am a heterosexual. It's something that I've wanted and needed since those childhood sexual events. How dare any lawmaker or politician try to make that illegal. It's healthcare. It's the freedom to choose. The freedom to be who I want to be. Nobody has a right to pass a law which prevents mental health experts from helping me to achieve happiness and contedness.

I found it hurtful that anyone would want to create a law banning conversion therapy. I still didn't fully understand my own past. I didn't understand what I had been through. I still couldn't begin to understand myself, my past, my trauma, and the many ways through which my own trauma had been used against me to re-victimize me. I didn't know. I didn't understand. I wasn't able to clearly see the allies and kindred persons who were working not to prevent me from getting therapeutic help but to ban others from being hurt the way that I was hurt.

I am once more reduced to tears, barely able to breathe, as I fully appreciate what those friends and allies have done. I didn't know. I couldn't know, because of how deeply programmed I was. My perspective was wrong. I couldn't see the ban, nor the form of therapy, for what they truly were.

Nobody was trying to pass a law to prevent me from getting the mental health services which I require. They wanted to pass laws which prevent that old preacher from teaching small children that 'God hates fags.' They want to protect other children from the pain, the trauma, the self-loathing, the decades of alcoholism and self-harm. They want to protect other children from the life that I have endured. For the first time in my life I am crying both tears of sadness and tears of joy simultaneously. As much as my childhood did cause me immense trauma, I can at least take comfort from witnessing an awakening throughout the world to protect children from this horrid harm and abuse.

During the pandemic I began struggling once again with my mental health. I had moved to a new town where I don't know anyone. It's a small place and it's hard to meet new people when everyone is trapped inside their home avoiding the coronavirus. The only way to meet new people was, embarrassingly, to use the Tinder app. I met a girl through Tinder who is several years younger than I am. Admittedly, I was quite nervous about meeting her for the first time. I was nervous for quite a few reasons, including several which are above and beyond the usual first date jitters.

I was scared that I would fall into bad behaviors pertaining to alcohol. It's still far too easy to see alcohol as being a solution or a partial remedy for anxiety. I was also worried about taking my Naltrexone around someone new. What if she asked me about this pill? It would be quite uncomfortable if she noticed that I need to take a pill an hour before a drink and that I'm restricted in how long after the pill I can continue to enjoy a glass of wine or a beer with her. Those are things which added to my nervousness and apprehension.

My biggest issue, though, was sex. She's in her mid-20s and we were meeting through Tinder. Is she expecting sex on the first date? While many men might have been hoping for that outcome, I certainly wasn't. To say that I'm shy about sex would be an enormous understatement. I'm a nervous wreck about having sex those first few times with someone new. Ever since my childhood experiences, I have struggled with feeling comfortable in my own skin. I'm uncomfortable being touched. If someone comes within a few feet of my body, I become tense and go into a heightened state of agitation. I feel threatened.

I don't want anyone to ever touch me.

How can I explain any of that to someone new? I didn't know how. I didn't know if I would need to. There was a lot running through my mind and my normal coping mechanisms are alcohol or avoidance. I couldn't do that this time. Not anymore. I was too lonely for too long and I needed to meet a new friend, and hopefully a new romantic partner.

I decided that I needed some help. I hired another therapist. I know that it may seem like overkill or that I'm being needy and dependent. I think I made the right decision in asking for some help from a qualified professional. In the end, I'm definitely glad that I sought some assistance. The new therapist I connected with is a very open-minded individual. She helped me to see things which, honestly, I just hadn't been able to see on my own.

I told the therapist about my history of alcohol abuse, taking Naltrexone, and about the childhood sexual experiences which had traumatized me. I admitted that a big part of why I was reaching out for help is because I was scared of being touched. Scared to have sex with the new girl I'd met on Tinder.

The therapist, whom I'll call Paulette, asked me to close my eyes and envision where the trauma 'lives' in my body. It was a bizarre question, though it immediately resonated with me. The trauma *does* live in my body. I can feel it. I know it's there. It's in my gut and it physically affects my body. It physically hurts me and causes monotonous digestive distress. Paulette went over a few breathing and positive thinking exercises which, normally I may have dismissed as whacko pseudo-science, but I'd decided to fully embrace.

One of Paulette's areas of expertise as a therapist is childhood trauma. Everything that I described to her from alcohol abuse, flinching when people come close to touching me, the fear over having sex with a new partner, were all things she almost expected me to describe. She'd seen it all before. The only difference that she seemed to note in my past was the religious indoctrination. That's what she zeroed in on right from the beginning.

Paulette explained 'conversion therapy' to me. She talked about how it had been banned in Canada and elsewhere. I still wasn't seeing what was right before my eyes until Paulette spelled it out for me.

"That is what was done to you," she said with a clear loathing toward the practice. "You were subjected to conversion therapy as a child."

I wasn't able to react right away. I was shocked, at first. Then it slowly began to click. They were worried that I'm gay. My parents walking toward us in the woods, back when I was with those other boys, they were close. They were so close, I remember it now. I was the only child in my family sent to the youth group. The only one sent to that old preacher to be indoctrinated to hate gay people. Only me. None of my other siblings were sent there. Why had the preacher sat me down and glared at me the way that he did, with those old hateful eyes, waiting for me to confess something? I understand it now. I understand why I was sent there and what it was intended to do.

They were worried that I'm gay and they sent me to conversion therapy.

That effort to indoctrinate me to make me hate gay people was the single worst thing that has ever happened to me in this world. It broke me. It destroyed so much of me. It permanently altered my perception of God, the meaning of life, and deprived me of my own sense of self. What they did to me was a horrible moral failing. An abuse. A crime. They taught me to hate all homosexuals. To condemn them. To loathe them. To forever look down upon them.

They taught me to hate myself, and called it love.

Chapter 15
Who am I?

The biggest question in my life for which I've always been too afraid to answer is obvious. Who am I? Am I gay? If I were gay, would that be okay? I don't know. I don't know who I am. I don't know the answers to any of those questions. Sure, I know the name on my birth certificate and I know who my parents are. Yet I don't truly know myself. I spent my entire childhood, youth, and early adult years not allowing myself to access the full range of my memories let alone genuinely consider the type of person that I am. If I am gay, it has been so completely buried behind wall after wall of inner psychological protections that I don't know if I'll ever truly be able to answer that question.

I honestly don't know if I'm gay or if I'm straight. I don't know if I am a good person or if I am so damaged that I am broken beyond repair. Part of me feels that I am not a good person. Guilt, shame, embarrassment, self-loathing, and a host of other profoundly negative emotions occupy enormous space in my mind at all times. My inner dialogue has been one of hatred toward myself and toward others with unlimited voraciousness. It was programmed into me as a hatred mandated by Almighty God, and as a true believer in God I have dedicated unlimited mental energy toward that hatred. It has utterly exhausted me. It has consumed me. It has deprived me of peace, contedness, and all manner of happiness.

I am so done with all of it. The hatred. The negativity. The darkness. I'm done. Here, now, henceforth. I am done with that dark past.

I began this story by telling you that this is a form of therapy for me. And it has been. It forced me to think through every part of my life story and to visualize the progression of events from the source of my mental illness to where I am today. I have a better understanding of myself now. I also want to help others to heal from their addiction and their trauma. I don't see my story as being inspiring, uplifting, or instilling a sense of positivity in others.

My story is one of survival, perseverance, and learning to love. I hope that some part of that translates into something constructive or useful for anyone who may have found this story. Whatever your personal challenges are in life, I hope that you find your own ways to overcome the negativity and to find your own happiness.

For me, I know that I want to have *life* after learning to exist in a zombie state for all those years. Sober, healthy, happy life.

I want to be a good person. I want to be a kind, compassionate, rational, level-headed person who would help others in times of need and look out for those around me. These are basic foundational attributes which most people in their thirties are able to determine about themselves. I'm still caught in some of the basic identity-type questions which many others sorted out in their teenage years.

Am I gay?

I don't believe so. I'm far too attracted to the beautiful women I meet to identify as gay. I know that I'm not 100% straight, though, either. I've never been able to determine how much of my sexual curiosity is genuine, rather than an after-effect of my childhood experiences. Am I only curious about these things because they hurt me and I'm still unable to process the pain? I don't know.

When I look at the world today I see children are being used as political pawns in an increasingly hostile and violent culture war. I find this profoundly sad and disappointing. If my own story teaches us anything it's that ideological indoctrination of children about sex, sexuality, or their identity can lead to lifelong and deeply painful forms of trauma. Let kids be kids. Let them be free of indoctrination and protect them from adults seeking to program them with an extremist point of view.

The ongoing battle to indoctrinate children runs the risk of creating more people like me who struggle with anxiety, depression, addiction, and identity crises. The pain is real and can often be unbearable. Why are we still allowing adults with extreme views to harm innocent children?

Once you program your young child with an ideology or an identity, that psychological encoding is there for life. There's no 'delete' button to de-indoctrinate a person at a later point in their life. Here I am nearly three decades later trying to answer the most basic questions about myself. I wouldn't wish this kind of disorientation and emptiness on anyone.

Parents, caregivers, educators: consider how your words, actions, and teachings could impact a young, impressionable child. Take steps to ensure you aren't the cause of some child's lifelong trauma. Don't indoctrinate children.

I am fortunate to have learned some healthy techniques for moving forward. I've had to learn how to accept and how to enjoy being intimately touched by a partner. I'm happy to say that I'm doing well with that. I am very fortunate to have found a partner who accepts me and is understanding of my traumatic past. Yes, it is the girl from Tinder, in case you were wondering! She tells me that she loves me every day now. I'm finally ready to accept that love and to see the positive qualities in myself that she sees.

My life has been a difficult journey. It has certainly had its share of tumultuous bumps and detours in the road. I've finally reached the point, through the help of Paulette and my new perspective on life, that it is time. It's time for me to heal. It's time for me to accept the events that I cannot change. It's time for me to shift my focus from past trauma to present, and future, happiness and solitude.

Some readers may wonder why I am not expressing some rebuke or profound disapproval with how my parents treated me. That's a valid question, in my view. There are a few additional details which may help readers to understand my parents. I would say that most importantly we need to consider their childhood experiences. Both of my parents had fathers who fought the Nazis tooth and nail across Europe. Both of them had many uncles and grand-uncles and other male relatives who went to fight the Nazis in the earlier days of World War II, and never returned.

My parents are each children of men who were traumatized by a horrific war. Their fathers returned from defeating Nazi Germany and were deeply scarred and wounded men. Their families mourned the loss of uncles, brothers, cousins, and others who died either in direct combat with Nazi forces on the battlefield or some who were captured by the Germans and never heard from again. My grandfathers fought through some of the most storied battles and campaigns of World War II, suffering every psychological wound one may expect from such a horrible chapter in human history.

I will not now nor will I ever speak one negative word about my grandfathers, those truly heroic men who helped to defeat Hitler and the Nazi empire. I simply am not blind to

the realities of how such men parented their own children –
my parents – and I am now able to recognize how the cycle
of trauma repeats itself, generation after generation. I don't
know the full story of my grandparents, my parents, or any of
those family members who came before me.

I can't condemn them for how they parented without
knowing the full truth of how they themselves had been
parented.

I wanted to tell my story for several reasons. Firstly, this
truly was a much-needed form of therapy for me. It helped
me to understand myself better and by organizing certain
events through this linear narrative I can more easily identify
the cause and effect and the full range of impacts I
experienced resulting from psychological trauma.

Secondly, I hope that my story helps others to understand
the devastation and destruction which can be done to a child
by indoctrinating them with an extreme, narrow view. The
significant majority of my life has been damaged and
negatively impacted more by the religious framing of my
childhood experiences than the experiences themselves.

Thirdly, I hope that my story and my message can help at least one other person out there. If your soul has been tormented as mine has suffered torment, if you have also spent a lifetime feeling an intense psychological pain without respite, if you have felt isolated, alone, misunderstood, and unloved by God for who you are: I see you. I hear you. I will share my love with you until you are able to love yourself for who you are.

I'm not ready to come out of my hiding place yet. I'm still hiding behind anonymity. This is my first time telling my story fully, completely, truthfully. As a person who has lived with great sorrow, Major Depressive Disorder, alcohol abuse disorder, anxiety, loneliness and persistent suicidal ideation I have simple words of wisdom for others on how to gain control over your life and find inner peace. It's all so simple that each of us has heard it a thousand times over, though many of us had our heads too perilously close to the surface of the water to allow the message to break through.

It really is quite simple: organize your space and keep surfaces clean and clear. Chop your own vegetables and eat healthy. If a podcast, newscast, or article is making you anxious or angry, set it aside. Choose not to allow someone else to bring negativity into your mind. Exercise, stretch your muscles, and breathe slowly. Grow your own plants and take pride in their growth. Be kind to animals, young children, and people who are far from home. Find a person who makes you laugh and encourages you to be the best possible version of yourself. Take ownership of your future and create the happiness you want to experience tomorrow. And on clear, starry nights look up at the sky and take a moment to ponder the vastness of space, life, and all the unseen wonders.

Humans are powerful beings. We have the ability to manifest our own happiness and positivity. Or should we lose sight of our goals, we can worsen our own heartaches and despair.

I was entombed by my own sadness for the majority of my life. This is the harm caused by conversion therapy. I understand that now. It has been a long, difficult, lonely path. In my heart I know that I was never truly alone. In those desperate dark moments God revealed his presence to me. He was always there with me in a conflicting duality. There was the Old Testament hate-monger the preacher had taught me to fear. That God was always there. Frightening me. Hating me. Then there was the true God. Accepting. Comforting. Guiding. I had been so completely programmed to believe in the hateful version of the Creator that only now, after a lifetime, has the cognitive dissonance begun to lift.

The two versions of God as I understood him are no longer needed. I don't need both of those comprehensions of God. I only need one.

God hates fags?

No, God doesn't *hate*. God *loves*. God is not an angry Sky Santa casting lightning bolts of hatred at the gays, or anyone else. God is that loving spirit who sees a person who is doing wrong. A person who is committing a crime by driving drunk. A person who has broken up a marriage, and created needless havoc and harm toward others. God sees you in your darkest moment, sitting alone drunk and descending further and further away. He sees you about to endure the worst humiliation of your life when he says *"I'll come sit in this car with you, tell you everything will be alright, and then you won't have to face this moment alone. You're scared and ashamed today, but I'll pick you up and make you whole again, better again. I will restore you."*

That's the God I know. There's no hatred anywhere in that God.

God loves me enough never to give up on me and to stick with me all these years – after all the mistakes that I've made. After all of my wrongdoings. He never forgot me. He didn't abandon me. After all these years and all of the pain and torture that I have endured, he whispers to me now that I never needed his forgiveness. He wants me to be who I am. He wants me to be happy. I know in my heart that he wants the same for you. He wants you to heal from those events which have scarred you. He wants you to embrace life and to find your own happiness, and to share your joy with others.

I spent a lifetime searching for divine loopholes or caveats. Anything that would absolve me of my sins and grant me forgiveness for things that happened when I was just a child. Only now do I realize that his forgiveness was so elusive because he'd never condemned me in the first place. Only a bitter old homophobic preacher, falsely speaking in God's name, had condemned me. Not God.

Listen to God. Not the bigots. Not the haters. Not those who want you to feel lesser than. God doesn't hate. God is love.

God's love knows no prejudice, preacher.

To my childhood self –
You are forgiven. You are free.

Chapter 16
The Next Chapter of Life